TRAILS OF TRAGEDY AND TRIUMPH

THE CONSEQUENCES OF WAR

Nikos Ligidakis

Nikos Ligidakis

Copyright 2018 by Nikos Ligidakis

All Rights Reserved.
No part of this book may be reproduced, stored in a retrieval system, or transmitted by any means, electronic, mechanical, photocopying, recording, or otherwise, without written permission from the publisher.

This book is based on a true story. To protect the privacy of individuals, some names have been changed, some characteristics have been revised and some dialogue has been recreated. All thoughts reflect the author's research recollections of experiences over time. All contents in this book are the responsibility and faults of the author.

ISBN 978-0-9786202-5-7
Library of Congress Control Number: 2018805436

Published by Inkwell Books LLC
10632 North Scottsdale Road, Unit 695
Scottsdale, AZ 85254
Tel. 480-315-3781
E-mail info@inkwellbooksllc.com
Website www.inkwellbooksllc.com

Trails of Tragedy and Triumph

Nikos Ligidakis

"As a writer, my aspiration has always been to share my perspective on what it means to be a human being, in all its complexities. I wanted to tell a story that reflects a comparative importance of political structures, religions and histories of the past. My books represents a lifelong dream of putting into narrative form, my many observations of the brilliance and kindness of the human spirit: people at their worst and people at their best. It is my intention to engage the reader in the process of observing history in both times past and in current day happenings for the sole purpose of gaining greater clarity in the shaping of one's own approach to life and the deepening of individual insight."

Nikos Ligidakis

Trails of Tragedy and Triumph

Nikos Ligidakis

This book is also a tribute to all unsung heroes who engaged in the controversial conflict we call war. It is about the men and women who came from the ranks of civil societies, who left families and jobs behind to fight in the wars that others created. It is about those who now history refers too with the anonymous word "troops."

Trails of Tragedy and Triumph

Contents

The Mission 1
Gates of Hell 13
Who's the Enemy 17
Land of Fury 25
On The Run.. 35
Turbulence 49
Friends For Life 53
Lost.. 59
The Calendar 67
Day Of Judgement... 79
Higher And Higher.. 89
Death In The Valley.. 95
No Mans Land.. 105
The Feast... 115
Deep Roots.. 125
Dance With Me... 133
Birds Of Passage... 141
Anticipation... 147
Another World.. 153
The Wanderers... 157
Liftoff... 163
Deliverance 167
Proud Moments.. 171
Civilized... 179
New Life.. 189
A Full Circle... 197
The Reunion.. 201
Eternal Dilemma... 207
About The Author.. 213

Trails of Tragedy and Triumph

1

THE MISSION

Layers of diaphanous darkness spread out on the cloudy sky over the military base on this remote land which was surrounded by olive and cypress trees. The shapes of a few rows of military bomber planes lined up in the tarmac were visible, some notably battered from enemy fire; others were undamaged. A group of airmen stepped out from their tents into the dawn and walked towards the fighter planes. Some strode fast, others with lethargic steps. For most of these men, it was just like another day on the job just another mission. Eventually, all of them reached their fighter plane and took their positions.

Clark Bailey, the radioman, inspected and tested his electronic components. Bombardier Manny Cardenas checked his Sperry bombsight at the bottom-front of the plane. The Sperry bombsight was built around the Sperry gyroscope which helped stabilize the plane. The gyroscope quickly corrected the plane's movements and kept the target in site.

The co-pilot Lieutenant George Poulos, visually checked to see that obstructions were clear of the propellers and powered up the engines. He called, "All clear" the check answer, "All clear" came from the flight engineer, to clear the way for pilot Lieutenant Andy Ryker to prepare for take off. The rest of the crew walked around the tight spaces of the aircraft, scrambling for their position.

The team of Lucky Lady was ready for their mission, details known only to the pilot, co-pilot, and navigator, Lieutenant, Bob Pastorelli.

The deafening sound of the B24 engines disturbed the quiet of the morning on Palm Sunday, April of 1944. The flight engineer, Chris Moody took his position as the gunner on the top turret. The bomb bay doors were cracked open to clear the gasoline fumes from the cabin. Movement inside the B24 while wearing full gear was notorious uncomfortable and cold drafts seemed to be everywhere.

As the sun was crawling up from the far horizon, the morning frost melted away on the fighter plane to reveal its name; Lucky Lady. Below the name, there was the image of a pretty blond girl, dressed in a bikini and rolling a pair of dice. The numbers on the two large dice were a five and a two – lucky seven. On the nose of the plane, there were two more sets of rolling dice; one set with the numbers six-and-one and the other with five-and-two.

As the engines powered up, the aircraft vibrated furiously and after laboring to escape the runway lifted its nose over the city of Lecce. Lucky Lady began to climb toward the heavens. Six other planes were lifted to follow Lucky Lady. As the bomber plane was lifted higher, the crew put on their oxygen masks.

The importance of providing oxygen systems in aircraft was realized during the European war of 1914. It was a time of rapid advances in aeronautical technology which resulted in successively more powerful aircraft, that were able to fly higher into the atmosphere. The oxygen helped the aviators flying at higher altitudes to remain alert and be able to function well while making life or death decisions. The need of oxygen for safe flights was determined to be at around fifteen thousand feet and beyond.

The navigator, Bob Pastorelli was now in a crouching position in the nose gunner turret, a dangerous place exposed to the open enemy fire. On the left waist gunner's position stood John Mueller and on the right, there was Bill Stoney.

At the belly of the plane, sitting in a fetal position, was the ball turret gunner Art Bauer, the smallest man in the crew. And in the lonely tail turret was Shaun O'Brien.

The crew, especially the left and right waist gunners were grateful for the warmth of their heated suits and boots, and though their tight-fitting oxygen mask were uncomfortable, it protected their faces from the cold air whipping through the plane.

Lucky Lady was on its way to Steyr, Austria, a five-hour one-way trip, to drop a load of five-hundred-pound bombs on the only ball bearing factory left in the Luftwaffe.

It was an essential target since the entire world of machinery ran on ball bearings. Without them, it was impossible to manufacture or repair equipment.

A huge thundercloud had broken up overnight. The plane lifted close to the thirty-thousand fleet and now was flying through scattered clouds over the Adriatic Sea and into Yugoslavia.

The air was frigid and hostile.

The men on the plane seemed physically relaxed, some a bit apprehensive, others in silent prayer. All of them have been on many mission before and they knew what was coming beyond the tiresome humming of the plane's engines. A couple of them, John Mueller and Chris Moody had spent a few weeks in the hospital with malaria. The irony was that they'd rather be up here than lying in that dank, dark, cement hospital, overcome with chills and fever and wrapped in the excruciating pain of malarial cramps.

A few hours had passed since they left the base when the urgent message came over the intercom.

"Enemy planes approaching at three o'clock."

The clear, loud voice in everyone's earphones snapped the men back to reality.

The three o'clock planes belonged to Bill Stoney, the gunner on the right side of the plane, and to Chris Moody, the top turret gunner. As soon as the enemy planes were in range, the B24 gunners started firing.

A voice in the intercom yelled, "He's going down!"

"More coming in at nine o'clock," yelled another voice.

The nine o'clock planes were the concern of John Mueller on the left and to Bob Pastorelli in the nose turret. There were three ME109s, approaching fast, like hawks in full dive; they came at Lucky Lady with guns blazing. Tracers of bullets racing out to meet the American fighter plane. The B24 gunners manning the gun turrets were under heavy attack - a prickly sensation surfaced from beneath their skin as the ME109 planes surrounded the American aircraft and attacked it in an ongoing assault of firepower. The twin fifty-caliber guns of John Mueller cut across the front of one ME109 and, when it came within his firing range, he fired several rounds. As soon as one plane left his firing range, another one took its place.

Mueller was hyped up with a torrent of adrenaline as images flooded his mind: Pearl Harbor and the American flag. The blood of freedom was awakened within him; so too was his courage.

More planes came into the right, close to Bill Stoney's firing range. He answered their attack with his fifty-caliber guns.

The firing was fast and furious and, as enemy planes flew out of the American gunner's range, more German planes came in with blazing guns aimed at the pretty lady rolling her dice.

It seemed that the Germans were playing hide-and-seek. The German pilots known for their great skill flew their aircrafts in with machine guns chattering and then quickly were out of range. The eyes of the American gunners scanned the sky for new targets. "Come on!" some of them challenged the enemy. They knew that the first outpouring of fire was an indication of the mayhem to come.

The skies were clear for a brief moment, and it was cold, unbearably cold, as the sub-zero wind screamed in the waist windows.

The American seven plane formation held their positions and their predetermined altitude as instructed. Lucky Lady's bombardier Manny Cardenas was concern about the sensitivity of the Sperry bombsights. Any change of position, altitude or speed could make the bombs miss their target.

The gunners braced themselves and concentrated their sight for targets. Hitting their target was a skillful act. The German fighter planes would change position every few seconds, using evasive action to avoid the American machine gun fire. The pilots of the planes, while fighting combat, never flew straight and level for more than a few seconds.

"Flak, eleven o'clock low," The voice of Lucky Lady's pilot came with an urging warning.

A stream of enemy tracer bullets, like small glowing white-hot balls of fire, went whizzing past Lucky Lady. Some fragments struck the aircraft, but there was no way, at this point, to evaluate any damage.

In addition to the fire from the German planes, the sky was blackened with exploding anti-aircraft shells fired from the ground. All hell had broken loose. The sky raged with exchanged fire from the American guns and those on the German planes. The German fighters flew through their flak to get to the Americans. Their ME109s were in and out like a flash, even when some of them sustained battle damage from their ground fire.

Lucky Lady was just about ten minutes from the mission target but, to the crew members, it seemed like an eternity. John Mueller, from the corner of his eye, saw black smoke tracing the sky. It came from the back of their formation.

"Charlie is going down!" he yelled. There was a mournful silence as the rest of the crew realized that one of their own, was spiraling human lives towards death.

Tail-end Charlie was a term given to the last airplane in a formation. The trailing plane was always the most vulnerable to enemy fire since there was no rear protection.

Charlie swayed in the air like an acrobat on a tightrope who has lost his balance. Those who had a moment or two to watch, held their breaths as Charlie's pilot fought for control. But, Charlie's nose turned down toward the ground. The plane disappeared from anyone's sight, leaving behind an ugly scar of thick black smoke on the face of the sky.

They prayed for the boys to escape and be safe, but everyone knew it was unlikely because the plane was engulfed in flames.

Tail-end Charlie was also a term used for the rear gunner. His turret was subject to the most violent attacks since the Luftwaffe fighter pilots preferred to attack from the rear of the American bomber planes. Lucky Lady's Shaun O'Brien was cramped into the tail turret with so little leg space.

The Germans had figured out that the ball bearing plant in Steyr was the objective target and they were defending it with great tenacity. Several more fighters returned to attack the American formation. The battle was furious. Flak burst all around the formation. Heavy ammunition struck Lucky Lady over and again. The chances of Lucky Lady surviving the onslaught were extremely slim. Pilot Andy Ryker turned the plane toward the target and in the mist of smoke and blazing bullets, dropped altitude. Behind them, another B24 from their formation went down. Between the inferno of machine gun fire, anti aircraft fire, and smoke there was no way to tell which one it was.

Lucky Lady was almost over the target. Ahead, meager sunlight reflected from a maze of red-tiled roofs. Through a slight haze, the bombardier, Manny Cardenas could see the target. Once they reached the target, he dropped their full load of bombs onto two sizable buildings. As soon as the bombs were away, the pilot banked left and started losing altitude, so they could gain airspeed and head for home.

There were four American planes left in their formation.

For a few moments, all was quiet. This allowed the crew members a little bit of time to celebrate the success of their mission. But suddenly seven German fighters came at the American formation, one of them was an M110, flying just outside of gun range. Swiftly, the pilot lowered the nose of his aircraft and released several air rockets. These were the first air-to-air rockets the Americans had seen in the war. The crew members of Lucky Lady felt stripped of protection. There was nothing but paper-thin aluminum sheet metal between those powerful explosions and them.

More enemy fighters approached from all angles; the sky was suddenly filled with German planes – they were everywhere! Enormous amounts of flak from the ground fire crossed the bullets coming from the German planes. The possibility of death was becoming a reality.

The men in the tail and ball turrets reported that several two-engine fighters were steadily firing into their formation. A German M110 was glued to Lucky Lady's left wing. One of the American P47 fighters was following him, trying to shoot him down.

The exchange of fire intensified. Flak exploded all around the sky. Then there was an abrupt jolt and an explosion as one of the air rockets hit Lucky Lady. The rocket head went through the number three engine, knocking it out and at the same time putting the number four engine out of commission. The rocket head was supposed to explode on impact; however, for some reason, it went through the wing and exploded some six yards after exiting the wing. Had it exploded on impact, the entire crew would have been incinerated.

It seemed that Lucky Lady was living up her name.

The aircraft dropped sharply, and all men aboard struggled to keep their balance. The right wing of Lucky Lady was severely damaged: engines three and four were out and the fuel lines to that wing were severed. A gas-vapor trail appeared behind the wing, and it looked a mile long.

Lucky Lady was going down.

On the left waist gunner position, John Mueller's fingers were still on the trigger of his machine gun. He struggled to stay on his feet and shoot at the enemy fighters picking away at their disabled aircraft. He knew the pilot and the co-pilot had both feet on the left rudder, pushing with all their might, but the plane was still staggering like a drunken sailor.

Just as quickly, the enemy fighters veered off; they had spotted another formation of American planes about a mile off. They were out of sight when Lucky Lady curved downward. At this point, some of the crew members pulled up the ball turret and got Art Bauer out and into the waist area where they all snapped their vest pack parachutes onto their harnesses. They could hear the screech of the two remaining engines roaring at full power struggling to keep their failing B24 aloft.

The pilot's voice filled their ears. "We are losing altitude five-hundred feet per minute." His voice was calm. Andy Ryker was trying to get them as far away from the target as possible before bailing out. But every second was a risk; the plane was quickly filling up with high-octane fumes. One spark and it would explode into a ball of fire, killing everyone on board.

It is an amazing feeling as you stand between life and death, between the real and the surreal. Every power, every emotion that you possess surpasses the normal, to cope with a reality that has gone beyond what was thought at that moment to be impossible. Suddenly the sound of bullets whined past Lucky Lady; a group of M110s had spotted the falling plane. They seemed to be on their way back to their base for refueling, but they took the time to make a few swipes at the limping aircraft. Somehow, they missed vital areas and that appeared to aggravate them. A couple of them broke from their formation to chase wounded Lucky Lady and to unleash a few more bullets at the defenseless plane before turning to rejoin their formation.

The entire crew was sweating the possibility that just one spark could ignite the gasoline vapor trailing inside the plane and they would be blown to pieces. On the way down the American crew spotted another formation of enemy planes headed their way. Lucky Lady was not one of their primary targets, but the Germans simply took some time to use it for target practice. The German gunners shot several holes in the fuselage. Miraculously none of the members of the American crew were seriously injured by the enemy fire.

Andy Ryker's voice came on again, "We are approaching six thousand feet. The range of mountains ahead are seven thousand feet." The crash was inevitable.

The "abandon ship" bell rang out. "May Day! May Day! Bail Out!" They all turned to the bottom escape hatch. John Mueller was the last one, three men were ahead of him. The seconds ticked away. The mountains loomed closer.

Mueller turned back to his gun position and he prepared to jump from his waist window, but, as soon as he put one foot out, enemy bullets ricocheted all around him. He hurriedly drew his foot back in. "What is wrong with them, shooting at people going down?" He was furious.

He grabbed his fifty-caliber gun. Holding steady, he looked out. He couldn't believe what he saw; there, several yards away, where two German fighters so close that they looked as if they were one enormous plane.

So close Mueller could see the pilot's oxygen masks; he let his ammunition fly. He knew instantly that he had hit the plane closest to him. A burst of flames and shrapnel scatter across the sky as the first plane went down, the other fighter moved in closer through fire and metal shards.

Mueller knew the mountains were getting closer to every passing moment. She was trembling as he swung his gun toward the second fighter and fired away until the gun overheated and locked up. As soon as his heavy barrage hit the enemy plane, black smoke began to pour from it. A moment later, the sky filled with debris and the defeated fighter's nose turned straight down into a death spiral engulfed in a ball of fire.

Trails of Tragedy and Triumph

2

GATES OF HELL

A strange sensation overcame John Mueller as two forces collided inside of him; joy and sadness. He wanted to scream for joy, from the glory that welled up inside of him, but he grieved for the lives lost.

Turning quickly, he saw that the bottom escape hatch was clear now and as the plane tilted for its final descent into the mountainside, he jumped to safety. Airmen are trained to count to ten before pulling the ripcord on their parachutes.

Mueller, sensing that the ground was coming closer, did not even count to one. He pulled the chord and the chute flew in his face, ripping off his hat and goggles. Flakes of mothballs flew into his nose, mouth and eyes, blinding and gagging him. He coughed and rubbed his eyes as his free-fall started to come under control. His eyes opened just in time to witness Lucky Lady falling out of control, trailed by thick, black smoke and then vanish into a ball of fire on the side of the snow-capped mountains. The smoke-filled sky was filled with open parachutes floating desperate men to safety, while airborne gunfights were raging all around them. Mueller was trying to guess if everyone from Lucky Lady had gotten out safely when a German fighter appeared to his right.

Mueller stared, wide-eyed, as the enemy plane made a pass

within a few feet of where he helplessly hung in the air currents. He braced himself for bullets or being run over. But, surprisingly the German pilot waved at him and like a good fellow, Mueller waved back. He didn't want any hard feelings with the German pilot who turned and made a second pass. The plane flew by so close it was almost touching Mueller's parachute. Suddenly the plane turned away, giving the parachute a prop wash. Mueller wondered if the pilot had done that on purpose and if his wave was a sarcastic goodbye. After the air wash, Mueller's parachute stretched out straight and started to collapse. The shroud lines were tangled and it was most likely they would not open again.

His free fall began, falling fast, buffeted by the wind whistling in his face. Mueller had just closed his eyes in despair when he was abruptly pulled upward. His eyes flew open and he was looking up into the graceful folds of his wide-open parachute spread out to hold him up - the sun showing through its canopy. He began to breathe again. As Mueller hung waiting for the ground to come up and meet him a visitor came by; it was a blackbird. The bird circled, checking him out. Mueller smiled at his black flying friend. Sounds of engines roared above his head. Gunfire chattered on the horizon. He could not tell what direction it was coming from. The blackbird swung around again, eying him with his head cocked to the side.

The blackbird flew away, abandoning him as he was falling into a strange land. While John Mueller was surrendering his fate to the unknown world below, memories of how he got here flashed in his mind.

It was Sunday, December 7, 1941, the day the Japanese attacked Pearl Harbor, he was with his friend Bill Stoney, sitting in their favorite diner in Freeport, Michigan. The two friends were working on the construction of a new bridge. John, was not at work that day due to a work-related injury. A while back, he was carrying a can full of boiling hot tar from the holding tank to the brick area and the handle of the can broke loose, spilling hot tar down his legs. It clung to his flesh, causing an intense third-degree burn. Finally, his legs were almost healed from the severe burn and he was about to return to work.

But, on Sunday morning, when the two friends heard the news about Pearl Harbor, work was the last thing on their mind.

The following morning, the two friends got into John's car and drove to the nearby recruiting office in Grand Rapids to sign up to serve their country. Meanwhile, details of the Pearl Harbor attack were being reported: The first attack came at 7:53 AM.

The quiet of the morning was shattered by machine gun fire coming from the Japanese airplanes, followed quickly by the sound of explosions. Within minutes, anti-aircraft guns returned the enemy fire. A bomb crashed through the two armored decks of the battleship, Arizona, igniting its magazine. The explosion ripped open the sides of the battleship. Within minutes the ship sank, taking one thousand-three-hundred lives with her. And that was just the first attack. The second wave of enemy planes came an hour later and by ten o'clock it was all over.

Approximately four hundred and sixty enemy airplanes had attacked Pearl Harbor. They destroyed one hundred and eighteen American planes, crippled or destroyed eighteen battleships, and left two thousand four hundred and three seamen dead and one thousand one hundred and seventy eight wounded.

In the meantime, the United States and Britain declared war on Japan and the Japanese promptly declared war on the United States and Britain. A few days later Germany and Italy declared war on the United States. Hitler had previously sought to avoid war with America while he was engaged in battle with Russia. The two friends enlisted and reported to Battle Creek for induction. From there, Bill Stoney was sent to the Jefferson Barracks in Missouri for basic training, while John Mueller was sent to the Greensboro Training Center in North Carolina. As they entered the gates of their training centers, they couldn't imagine that these gates would take them to hell on earth.

They were twenty-one years old.

3

WHO'S THE ENEMY

John Mueller squinted his eyes against the sunlight reflected in the snow. From the south, a group of men were running like ants on a hill in his direction A few motorcycle riders were racing along with them on the narrow side of the road. Another group of people came running through a canyon from the north.

Mueller couldn't tell if they were enemies or friends. He had to assumed they were all enemies. He prayed for a quicker descent so he could run before the enemy got to him.

Mueller was already planning his escape route – he was going to run east, parallel to the mountains. As soon as his feet hit the ground, he would start running between the two groups who were racing to capture or to kill him.

It was an unfair race between a slow floating parachute and fast approaching enemies.

He finally landed on a snowy slope. The landing was hard, he fell on his back and began sliding down towards the bottom of a small hill. He felt no pain while he was falling down the hill his mind was preoccupied with how to escape. His sliding and rolling went on for about fifty feet. Once he hit the bottom of the hill, he stood up and hurriedly unfastened his chute. He looked around at the unfamiliar landscape and suddenly felt as though he had fallen back in time to a place before man's coming, an age-old land of danger and death.

People yelling from the north drew his attention. Mueller now realized that they were German soldiers, coming for him and about a quarter of a mile away. Running north was out of the question. Muller turned to run eastwards, but it was too late. A man was standing at the top of the hill from where he had slid down. This unusual man was pointing his machine gun at Mueller.

"*Ruskie!*" he yelled in a commanding voice, as his gun was leveled at Muller's chest.

John Mueller sucked a huge gulp of cold air and put up his hands.

"No! No! Americano!" he cried.

The rebel did not lower his gun. Muller waited, hoping that he was an American sympathizer. He was aware that there were Yugoslavian guerrilla fighters friendly to the Allies, but there were also guerrilla fighters helping the Germans.

A woman along with three other men appeared at the top of the slope and stood behind the man with the machine gun. The rebel who showed up first slid down the bank and rose a few feet from Mueller. He was a big man, over six feet tall, unshaven, with clothes soiled from long travels. Suddenly, Mueller noticed his left sleeve was empty - his arm was missing. Mueller braced himself; he did not know what to expect. The rugged rebel slung his gun across his shoulder, hugged and kissed Mueller on both cheeks. Mueller welcomed that hug and sighed in relief. Once Mueller realized that these rebels were friends, he handed his 45-caliber handgun to their leader. As he had been instructed in training to do if he met friendly forces.

The rest of the rebels ran down the slope. Quickly they picked up the chute and ran back up into the canyon. They motioned for Muller to follow. The rebels ran and Mueller followed.

Beyond the hill, the rebels ran into a narrow, long canyon, strewn with rocks and boulders. The canyon seemed empty at first, but suddenly more men and a woman rebels appeared from behind the rocks to join them. There was no time for introductions. The newcomers joined and they all ran down the narrow gorge, between and over rocks, tramping through the snow, always looking behind and above. Suddenly, above them, they spied moving silhouettes. Urgent commands, in a language unfamiliar to Mueller, indicated the danger was coming their way. Soon, heavy machine gun fire rained down, aimed at them. The Rebels jumped to the sides of the canyons and took cover behind rocks and returned fire. The sounds from the guns and grenades echoed in the canyon walls and created deafening mayhem Not knowing what to call his rescuer Mueller gave the one-armed man the nickname Machine Gun. The one-arm rebel fighter grabbed Mueller, pointed to a hole between the rocks and motioned for him to crawl into it.

The Germans had abandoned the rim and entered the canyon. They were moving up behind the rebels, going from rock to rock, moving steadily toward the hidden band of the rebels.

Machine Gun was standing next to Mueller's hiding place. He glanced at him. His face was calm. He nodded his head pointed at himself and gave thumbs up in reassurance. "We are going to be okay. I've done this many times," he seemed to say.

Mueller tried to stay calm.

Machine Gun gave a hand signal to his band of rebels. A few of his men and women raced up and threw grenades into the cluster of advancing German soldiers. The Germans answered with machine gun fire.

The explosions and gunfire reverberated in the canyon. The gunfire continued, now from both sides. Bullets scraped the rocks around Muller. Ricochets zinged through the air.

Mueller watched Machine Gun with amazement and admiration. With one arm, he handled his gun with mastery and accuracy. The guerrillas tossed more grenades. Rocky earth, stones and dirt flew up, mingled with helmets, clothing and body parts of German soldiers. Then there was quiet.

The rebels cautiously came out of hiding. A few of them moved up the sides of the canyon, where several dead Germans lay, and spat on the ground, murmuring words Mueller did not understand. Machine Gun tapped Muller on the back, cracked his mouth into what could have been a smile, and shouted an order. Time to move out. All rebels were accounted for and none were seriously injured.

Mueller was walking next to the one-armed rebel, he pointed at him and said Machine Gun. The rebel gave him a puzzled look and lifted his shoulders slightly.

Mueller pointed to the one-arm rebel's gun and said, "machine gun" then pointed at him. He repeated his gestures, pointed to the machine gun, then pointed at the rebel. The rebel opened his eyes wide, pointed at himself and said, "machine gun." He got it. "Yes, yes," he exclaimed nodding his head in satisfaction. He liked his nickname.

As they marched, Mueller took a good look at the people who had just saved his life. Their clothes were worn and ragged. Their faces and eyes were dark and intense. Most of the men had beards; the rest had several days of unshaven growth. The women were dressed like the men, with their hair hidden under army style hats. All could climb like antelopes, as he would find out while their journey together continued. Mueller stood just five-and-a-half feet tall, with a well-built upper body from working construction jobs. He had a difficult time keeping up.

From time to time, one of the rebels would glance back to make sure they were not followed. Mueller wondered what cause they were fighting for? All he knew was, at that moment, they were not against him. He was extremely thankful for that.

At this stage of World War II, Yugoslavia was divided into several cliques of guerrilla warfare. The main bands were the Partisans of Tito and the Chetniks of Mihailovic. After April 17, 1941, when Yugoslavian High Command surrendered to the Germans at Sarajevo, Colonel Draza Mihailovic and his band of mostly Serbian rebels reached Ravna Gora on the western slopes of the Suvobor Mountains in Serbia, and there he established his headquarters. At this time the Allies supported the resistance movement led by Mihailovic.

The Germans responded by forming the Prinz Eugen SS Division to engage the resistance movements. The troops in Prinz Eugen massacred Serbian civilians as collective punishment for supporting resistance movements. Entire Serbian orthodox villages were burned down and the inhabitants, men, women, and children, were shot.

The harsh German occupation left the Serbians in a dilemma. Some wanted a temporary armistice with Germany to end the reprisal massacres of Serbians, but Mihailovic decided to keep his forces intact and wait for the Allied landing. However, as Tito's Partisan troops were increasing in numbers, the British aid began to abandon the Chetniks and shifted their support to the communist-led Partisans.

Josip Broz, known first as Tito, was a sergeant in the Austria-Hungarian army and fought against the Serbian military during World War I. Broz became a prisoner of war in Russia, where he adopted the policies of the Bolshevik Regime of Vladimir Stalin and returned to Yugoslavia a staunch communist. He eventually became the Secretary-General of the Communist Party of Yugoslavia. When the country fell apart in 1941, Tito saw an opportunity to seize power. There was little Partisan activity in the fall of Yugoslavia in April 1941 and during the surprise German attack on the Soviet Union in June. It was evident that the communists gathered their strength to help the Soviet Union that now was in danger.

Partisan activity began in Northwest Serbia using mines and committing acts of sabotage against bridges and telephone lines. There were additional attacks on convoys and raids on police stations and banks to obtain arms and money. The Germans treated the Partisans as criminals. They took no prisoners and punished civilian populations suspected of helping partisans.

The Partisans also discarded the laws of war. They attacked German hospitals and ambulance convoys and stole medical supplies after killing wounded Germans. They also adopted the no prisoner policy. Yugoslavia now was a country divided: Mihailovic made clear his Serbian politics and anti-communist stance. He considered Tito a traitor and a threat to the Serbian-run Yugoslavian Kingdom and felt his next duty was to crush him. In his zeal to defeat Tito, coupled with the betrayal of his loyalty from the Allies, he made a deal with the Germans, offering a truce in return for arms and the commitment to fight Tito's rebels.

As the fight between the two factions escalated, Tito's Partisans moved out of Serbia and made their main base in the high mountains of Bosnia. They remained there during most of the war. Mihailovic's Chetniks remained in Serbia during the rest of the occupation and maintained truces with the Germans and Italians.

By 1943, the Partisans had sixty-thousand men in the field. When Italy left the war, Tito's Partisans forces seized the weapons of six Italian divisions, while two other Italian divisions joined the Chetnik forces. Partisan armed strength rose to two-hundred thousand rebels; it was then when Churchill decided to back Tito instead of Mihailovic. By the end of 1944, the Partisan numbers of rebels were doubled and became an immense force.

Mueller was now traveling with a small band of rebels. They did not speak English, and though he still did not know where they were leading him, he felt relatively safe. He was uncertain how much farther they would travel this day, but he wished it would not be far to food and shelter. He was not sure his strength would hold up much longer.

At least the rays from the setting sun brought some warmth in the freezing air. A bright palette of colors of lavender, orange, and brilliant yellow penetrated through the low-hanging clouds on the horizon as the sun tilted away.

The sun was about to set on this day, a day he had been as close to his death as he had ever been.

Trails of Tragedy and Triumph

4

LAND OF FURY

The pilot of Lucky Lady, Andy Ryker, thought that all the men had jumped off the plane to their safety. Therefore, he too abandoned the falling aircraft. He was unaware that Mueller was left behind.

Andy's parachute veered towards an area full of citrus trees. It was headed for a rough landing. His feet hit the top of a tree. The chords of his parachute tangled into the branches and sent him rolling on the ground and finally landing against a tree trunk. Then there was darkness.

Over a transparent fog and beyond the deep-green leaves of the citrus trees, there was a beautiful sunset. Ryker was certain he was in heaven. Strange sounds of human voices buzzed in his ears. He saw weather-beaten faces of men wearing bandoleers over their peculiar clothing. They were engaged in an animated argument. "What kind of heaven is this?" - he thought.

The fogginess cleared, his eyes opened wide, the sound of the voices stopped and the eyes of four sturdy faced men were looking at him. After a moment of silence, the men began talking again, slower this time. "I don't know what you are saying." Ryker interrupted them. The four-man looked at each other, then turned to Ryker and one of them said, "Okay, okay."

Excruciating pain penetrated Ryker's body as he tried to stand up. One of the rebels said something while gesturing with the palms of his hands. He signaled Ryker to stand still. He then pointed to Ryker's ankles. Both of his ankles were possibly broken, the pain now was unbearable. One of the men took a bottle of clear liquid out of his backpack and urged Ryker to drink. After the first gulp, Ryker's face almost exploded. The liquid was rakija, a strong fermented drink made of various fruits, a favorite in the Yugoslavian region. The rebels had a good laugh over Ryker's reaction and urged him to drink more. "Why not," Ryker said and gulped some more rakija. Surprisingly the liquid eased up his pain a bit. In the meantime, the rebels cut off a few branches from the trees, smoothed them with their knives, took some rope out of their bags and made a stretcher.

Meanwhile, as the sun deepened into the horizon, there was concern in the German barracks because one of the patrols had failed to report back to their base.

A rescue team was dispatched from the base to search for the missing group.

Just before darkness, the rescuers entered the canyon and as they walked deeper into the ravine, they discovered the lifeless, mutilated bodies of their fallen comrades. Filled with fury, they radioed their base and were told to follow the rebels and kill them. They were also told to kill any Americans they are harboring.

Mueller was trying to keep up with the footsteps left on the snow by the striding rebels who were trying desperately to get out of the canyon. Beyond the canyon, tiny lights blinked in the dusk. It was the German camp, so far away but yet, so noticeably near. The rebels ahead of him marched on as the darkness of the night overtook them.

The moon was hiding behind thick clouds as Mueller followed the faded shadows of the rebels. The sounds of their boots crushing the snow assured Mueller that he kept pace with the rebels. After a few hours, they reached the top of a snow-covered mountain. The clouds had now cleared the sky and the moon rose above them, mute and half round.

The team of rebels headed down the other side of the mountain, the snow now glistened pale blue under the moonlight, illuminating their path all the way to the plains below.

Mueller thought about his friends. Wondering if they were dead or alive, free or captured.

Mueller's feet slipped on the icy snow as he tried to keep up with his protectors.

He walked fast and seemed unwearied. They knew what Mueller did not know - the Germans were pursuing them. His legs and body ached and he desperately wanted to sit down and rest. But the tireless rebels had no intention of stopping. Occasionally, one of them would glance back to be sure that Mueller was following.

They kept walking long into the night trying to put distance between the Germans.

As the hours passed, the only sound was that of their labored breathing and the crunch of their boots in the snow.

It was near midnight when Mueller saw a scattering of lights ahead to his left, on the bottom of the slope they were now trekking. The rebels headed toward the lights. Soon they entered a village etched on the rocky surface of the mountains, hidden among trees.

As they walked down the narrow, muddy streets, the rebels

were greeted with evident admiration. Women reached out to clasp their hands. Men cheered them on from the doorsteps of the humble homes. There were about a hundred people in the village, all dressed in heavy winter coats and hats.

Mueller was led to a large hall in a building in the middle of the village. The inside of the home was simple, with a roof of exposed beams and a brushed dirt floor.

There was a wood-burning stove in the center and the entire space was draped in warmth. There was a desk with a few faded, leather chairs, and a stairway leading to an upstairs floor. Guns and ammunition rested against one of the walls.

Mueller was offered one of the leather chairs and sank into it gratefully. He closed his eyes and drifted off in the warmth of the room.

Earlier in the afternoon, George Poulos was picked up by two rebels and brought to the cave-like impression on the wall of a canyon and he was told to wait there. Pressing flat against the mountain he soon heard deafening shots and explosions. One by one the rebels brought Pastorelli, Bailey, Bauer, O'Brien, and Moody to the mountain side. Part of the team was reunited. They exchanged stories of how they were picked up to safety by the rebels and prayed for rest of the Americans to be safe. They squeezed into their narrow cavern, awaiting their fate in this strange land. Sounds of gunshots, hand-grenade explosions and intense shouting, created mayhem around the Americans.

All of the sudden there was silence. An anxious quietness dispersed across the canyon just before nightfall. The four rebels signaled to the Americans to sit still and wait. None of them spoke English so communication was through hand gestures and facial expressions. The four rebels were anxiously looking towards the canyon. A notable sigh of relief appeared on their faces when they saw another group of rebels coming their way. Among them were Stoney and Cardenas. After engaging in an animated but whispered conversation, some pointed towards the mountain and others pointed towards the outlet of the canyon. Finally, they signaled the Americans to stand up and follow them towards the exit of the canyon. As they quietly walked out of the canyon, brushing against the mountainside, voices of German commands sounded in the distant mountain slopes.

Mueller was about to fall asleep when the door of the warm room opened. The blast of cold air woke him up. Two rebels entered first but soon followed by his friends. They were all exhausted and cold but alive, all except for Ryker.

Clark Bailey said he saw Ryker's parachute coming out of the plane, but lost track of him as he drifted farther away. Others confirmed they had seen Ryker escape the flaming Lucky Lady.

They hoped for the best as they gathered around the stove and exchanged stories.

The rebels had rescued every one of them from German capture and, looking around at each other as they talked, they knew they were alive because of this brave, radical group. As time passed, their voices gradually faded, and they began to reflect on how they survived this day and what might be ahead of them at daylight.

The rebels had been murmuring amongst themselves during the reunion. Once the Americans were settled, the rebels offered them a bowl of polenta and a cup of water to wash it down. Everyone tore into the meal hungrily. They had gone many hours without eating and so, too, it appeared, had their rescuers. After collecting their bowls and cups, the rebels indicated they should get some rest. The Americans stretched out on the floor around the room, and soon they were all asleep.

A few hours before sunrise the American's slumber was interrupted by the sound of the door opening with another blast of cold air and urgent voices. Two rebels came in carrying Andy Ryker on a stretcher. He was conscious, and he gasped and grimaced with pain as the rebels lifted him into a chair. His ankles were swollen like large potatoes.

He opened his eyes and looked around, taking in the expressions of worry and concern on his friend's faces and so he grimaced a smile. His pain was obvious, but he was glad to see all of them safe.

The entire team relaxed now they had been reunited and gathered around Ryker. "Watch the feet. Watch the feet," he warned.

Ryker told his friends that he was impressed with the rebels. They had taken turns carrying him, sometimes on their backs while running and exchanging gunfire with the Germans. They had succeeded in shaking off their pursuers and continued the fast pace for several miles before they were able to slow down their pace.

Once they felt they were relatively safe, the rebels put Ryker back on the makeshift stretcher and carried him over the mountains and down into this little village.

Ryker glanced over to the rebels as they entered and departed the room.

The faces of the rebels were hardened and determined; men and women who had become accustomed to hunger, cold, and a life on the run.

Their passionate spirits were rooted in this wild, rocky

earth of their homeland, they clung to it and protected it fiercely. Their expressions seemed to say - We will fight, here and now.

"They are my new heroes," Ryker said.

One of the rebels, followed by a villager, approached the American group. The man from the village knelt by Ryker's feet and gingerly pressed his fingers into the flesh around his feet and ankles. He seemed to be the village doctor. He looked up at Ryker's face and then reached out to pat his hand in a gesture of reassurance. He uttered a few orders in a low voice to the rebels who looked on. The rebels signaled to the Americans for help to hold Ryker still. Five Americans held him tightly by the arms, legs and body. Ryker took a deep breath and nodded to the doctor.

The doctor grasped the heels and arch of Ryker's foot and quickly jerked on it. There was a cracking noise and Ryker yelled loudly. The doctor did not waste any time. He immediately moved to the other foot and repeated the procedure. Before Ryker could even take another breath, the other ankle had also been set back into place.

The angles were not broken as first thought by the rebels but dislocated.

Ryker slumped down, sweating and breathing heavily. Muller said, "It's okay Andy, it's over." Ryker slowly opened his eyes; there was a wisp of relief. Then his eyes closed with a heavy sigh.

Suddenly, an explosion ripped through the night. Everyone in the room, except Ryker, who was nearly unconscious, jumped at the sound of mortar shells hitting the mountain.

Several rebels rushed into the room from outside; they grabbed their gear and guns and signaled to Americans that it was time to leave.

They put Ryker back on the stretcher and moved out following the rebels.

Outside, mortar shells fell above and below the village.

They were coming from the other side of the mountain. Some hit the top of the mountain, sending flying rocks into the houses and buildings. A continued onslaught of mortar shells was flying around the village, onto the slopes of the mountain and on the opposite side of the narrow, uninhabited valley below.

The Germans were trying to shell the village from the valley the running rebels just left behind, but the village was protected in the leeward of the mountain. Rebels and Americans moved out into the dark, hurrying through the village and out onto the mountainside. They hunched down as rocks rained down upon them from the mountain explosions.

Flashes of white light from the explosions lighten the darkness while Ryker moaned in his dark dreams of semi-consciousness.

A faint gray light was appearing in the eastern sky above the rim of the dark mountains. Someone said that he thought he heard the crow of a rooster as they left the village behind them.

There were fifteen in this group. Four new faces of rebels, and one familiar face - the face of Machine Gun who again led the team. There were traveling fast, nearly at a run. The morning frost covered the trees and shrubs and added a glistening layer to the days-old snow.

Once out of the range of artillery, they headed for the upper reaches of the mountain, staying just below the ridge, and fled along the steep slopes. They had been traveling about an hour when the sounds of the exploding artillery stopped.

The soles of Mueller's and Bill Stoney's military boots

were beginning to break away; they were not made for a long trek by foot.

The fiery edge of the sun was now showing up over the mountains. The air temperature began to warm, imperceptibly at first, then more noticeably. The sound of measured drips came from the trees as the snow began to melt slowly. Their breath still clouded in the air.

They heard the sound of a machine gun fire in the distance, coming from the village they had left behind. The crew of Lucky Lady all hesitated for a second, looking back. The rebels grabbed their arms, shook their heads and urged them to move on. The next sound they heard was the sound of German aircraft. The Germans were attacking the village by air and land. Now, listening to the sounds of the attack, everyone's mind was with the rebels left behind, those who saved the American's lives yesterday, the ones who had fed them polenta, and all the women and children who were so kind to them.

There were some wet eyes in the group running for safety.

The Americans took turns carrying Ryker. "I am sorry you guys have to carry me." he kept saying. They all knew that they were alive because of Ryker who managed to keep the plane in the air long enough for them to bail out. He was the real hero among them. As they spent more time with the rebels, the Americans came to understand that these guerrilla fighters were holding the mountains of Yugoslavia, while the Germans occupied the valleys. The Germans could and did enter the mountains but at high risk of being killed. They did not have enough troops to secure the mountains and retain control of the valleys. The group marched on and the sun rose into a bank of clouds that was spread across the sky. Ryker dozed, and everyone tramped on silently, each lost in their thoughts. The bright sun midway its journey on the sky was now veiled by thick layers of clouds. There was a sound of a plane, somewhere far behind them. Machine Gun yelled an order and signaled for them to take cover. They ran into the shadows of large boulders, thick bushes, and under trees, and froze there like frightened rabbits. They held their breath as the German plane flew over them, low and slow. No one moved a muscle as the plane went past and seemed to be heading off to continue its search of the mountains. But, then the plane turned, circled and headed toward them again. The German plane approached, and time seemed to move slow. The rumble of the plane's engines grew louder, sweat ran over faces, eyes closed tightly, bodies froze, bracing for bombs and machine gun fire from the air as the plane seemed to be hovering right over their heads. Only when they realized that the sound of the engines had dwindled into the distance did they dare to breathe in relief.

At a command from Machine Gun, they all staggered out of their hiding places, faces showing strain and relief. Many continued to look apprehensively into the sky as they once again took up their march. The Americans still did not know where the rebels were taking them. They had no choice but to follow and trust their combat skills and their knowledge of the land and of the enemy. The Americans were entirely at their mercy, their lives in rebel's hands, walking in loneliness on this unfamiliar territory. They marched into the sunset. It was their second day behind enemy lines.

5

ON THE RUN

An empty, powerless feeling overcame Andy Ryker as he watched his friends carry him on a stretcher while climbing towards the mountaintops and laboring to keep up with their leaders. He knew that those who were trying to bring him to safety had to endure hunger, thirst, and exhaustion. It wasn't Ryker's nature to be helpless or to follow the footsteps of others. His mind traveled back to when he was a freshman in college, to another time that he was carried off the football field on a stretcher. He had an injury that almost ended his football career. Andy Ryker was the prototype image of the American Golden Boy; a charismatic quarterback, strong, blond hair, blue eyes, smart, polite and a great sense of humor. While playing football in college, he seemed humanly perfect. However, despite the encouragement of his coaches play professional football, Andy wasn't interested in a career in sports. He wanted to follow his other passion; flying airplanes. As an athlete, he could have gone quickly into a professional team. He could have been anything he wanted to be, but he chose to enlist in the military and fly warplanes. He chose to leave behind glory and wealth behind and serve his country. During the so-called Roaring Twenties, the economy was booming in Los Angeles. Andy's father, James

Ryker, a real estate investor, made several successful investments in the film industry and the family's wealth flourished. This was the period of American history known as the Prohibition, and alcohol had been declared illegal. The increase of the illicit production and sale of liquor was known as bootlegging. It also led to the infamous drinking spots known as speakeasies. The related rise in gang violence and other crimes produced a decrease in support for Prohibition by the end of the 1920s. At this time the United States was on the threshold of economic expansion and James Ryker was riding the wave of prosperity. Andy's mother, Lily, was part of the high society of Los Angeles.

The Rykers built a beautiful mansion in Hancock Park, an affluent residential neighborhood in central Los Angeles which featured architecturally distinctive homes. Everything seemed to be moving along with the Ryker family until the Great Depression hit the country and America spun out of control into an economic downturn. On October 24th, 1929, the stock market crashed and wiped out savings of millions of investors. Soon after the Depression began, consumer spending and investments dropped, causing steep declines in industrial output and rising levels of unemployment. With income inequality, there was a chaotic schism between plutocrats and hard times. Eventually, America would be drawn into the second World War and jobs would be created while wealth would be compressed.

James Ryker was one of the millions who lost most of his money during the Depression. It was a time of survival and scarcity. The Roaring Twenties were muzzled, and luxuries and frivolous spending were no longer possible. Eventually, the Rykers were forced to move out of their mansion in Hancock Park and move into Brentwood Hills. Their fancy cars, the Buick Marquette and

Chrysler Roadster, were reduced to a Model B Ford. They had to let go of the house helpers and to make agonizing readjustments. However, for Andy, it was like breaking into a new life of freedom. He was away from the life of high society, golf clubs and cocktail parties. He was living now around real people who struggled to survive. He felt sorry for his parents because he saw the quiet desperation in their faces. They had lost so much during the Depression, yet they remained stoic and resolved to overcome their enormous economic setbacks. The move to the new house on top of the hill in Brentwood brought the family closer together because they were living in a smaller house and had no household help. His mother now did the cooking, the dishes and many other household chores. His father had to go out to work. There was a spectacular view from the hill. There was greenery extending far into the distance and dropping just before the endless ocean. Being carried on the trails of the Yugoslavian mountains, Andy reminisced about the road which started at the top of the hill and curved down all the way to Sunset Boulevard.

The family seemed to be adjusting well, and in fact, grew to love this new location. Brentwood was not considered to be a swinging town, but it was beautiful. For Andy, growing up in this new environment gave him the opportunity to explore new and fascinating things. There were other kids in the neighborhood and he soon made new, inseparable friends. Andy and his friends created their own entertainment. Andy was an only child and, before moving to Brentwood, his life was spent around gardeners, housekeepers and private chauffeurs. His father pushed him to be the best in sports, but Andy wasn't interested. Andy Ryker was always looking up, dreaming of battling aircrafts in dogfights, saving lives in grueling airlifts, or flying dangerous missions deep into enemy territory. At a young age, Andy was inspired by barnstormers and the legendary World War I fighter pilots. On his tenth birthday, Andy convinced his parents to let him fly with an instructor. At the age of thirteen Andy Ryker was allowed to take lessons in an aviation school in Ventura. When War World II broke out, Andy Ryker volunteered for his duties and he went to San Antonio, Texas to do his flight training. With World War II raging, Andy found himself in the cockpits of bomber aircrafts.

The trail leading up and down the mountains were rarely marked. Anyone unfamiliar with the territory could easily get lost, but the rebels seemed to know the terrain well and seldom faltered in their march. It was early spring. At lower altitudes, green blades of grass were pushing up the earth and the wildflowers peeped from beneath the stones. Trees were blossoming, and birds were flying home on the heels of winter. Up in the high passes, the snow was beginning to melt. The aromas of spring were carried on a strong breeze, all the way up to the high trails they were climbing.

Two days had passed, two days of trekking mountains and through woods with no foods and very little water. The men often dug in the snow to get some clean water to quench their thirst. The rebels had small teams stationed on strategic lookout posts throughout the mountain. When they reached one of these posts, the team of escorts would change - fresh legs for tired ones. At one of these outposts, the Americans said goodbye to Machine Gun. The men had rested for a few minutes, and when the rebels motioned to the Americans that it was time to depart, Machine Gun did not don his gear. It took Mueller a moment to realize that he was staying behind. As they were departing, Machine Gun looked at Mueller with a sober expression. Mueller gazed back, not knowing how to thank this man for saving his life.

Finally, Mueller stood at attention and saluted the man who not only helped him but also traveled so far to ensure that the crew of Lucky Lady was safe. Machine Gun's eyes shone as he returned the gesture in rebel fashion; his fist tapped on his chest above his heart. The Americans turned and headed off once again into the mountains. Their destination remained unrevealed by their guides. As far as they knew, none of the rebels spoke English, and they did not see them take out any maps so that the Americans might be able to get a glimpse of any location. For purposes of necessity and survival, the Americans placed a blind trust in these war-worn people and trudged on.

The weather had warmed enough to make their flight suits uncomfortably warm during the day. Their feet began to sweat, and their boots heated up. Bill Stoney's soles were now flapping freely and when they stuck to his sweaty feet, they cause him to trip. In addition, after the sun went down, the temperatures dropped drastically, and the night air was freezing. The men would lie on the ground without covers and shiver in their suits. The Americans talked little amongst themselves. It was necessary to save most of their strength for the march. The silence was occasionally broken by Ryker who would say, "Let me walk, please, I can walk." As soon as those who carried him would stop, Ryker would try to place his feet on the ground and stand, but then he would give in to pain and frustration.

The Americans kept walking on – to the unknown. The third day, Mueller and Stoney were carrying Ryker's stretcher. Stoney was handling the back end. Every step he took was with great effort. He could hardly keep his balance because of his tripping on the flapping soles of his boots.

"John, hold up," he yelled at Mueller. As they stopped and placed the stretcher on the ground, he unfastened his boots, took them off and held them up. The sun glinted through the gaping holes in the soles, he shook his head and then threw the boots off into the brush at the side of the trail.

"You can't walk barefooted," Ryker said.

"I can't walk with those boots either," Stoney replied.

He was inspecting what was left of his socks when he heard a grunt, and someone called out, "Andy!" He looked over and Andy Ryker had rolled off the stretcher onto the wet ground. Stoney watched Ryker slowly lifted himself up, holding on to the trunk of a tree. He managed a grim smile.

Andy Ryker was of German descent and he told the rest of the crew that, "If you don't let me walk, I am going to dump you into the fatherland when we fly over Germany."

The crew just laughed, knowing the Ryker was from California. Now, they walked side by side, Stoney in his socks while Ryker used a tree branch as a cane. It was not long before sharp rocks and thorns had cut into Stoney's feet and tore more holes in his socks. He wondered if he had been rash in throwing away his boots. Ryker's ankles began to swell again, and within a few hours, they ballooned to twice their average size.

Everyone on the team was tired, thirsty and hungry. Their faces were red with exertion and the heat made their walk miserable. Some members of the team had cut off the legs of their flight suit and were rewarded with a mild breeze against their bare flesh. The sun began to sink behind the peaks of the mountains and darkness began to cover the earth. They turned a corner on the trail and saw a tiny village ahead, on the slope below. There were only a few homes, and they all seemed dark and uninhabited.

Once they arrived in the village, the Americans were divided into various homes to rest and again they were given polenta and water. The women of the village washed the blood off Stoney's feet with a wet cloth. He was in the room with Cardenas and Bailey. Suddenly the door flew open and a man entered.

"Hey, boys! How are you?"

At first, they could not believe what they were hearing; English! One of the rebels in the tiny village spoke English. The Americans began firing questions at him which he attempted to answer in his thick accent. He was a man of medium height, about fifty years old, dressed in the familiar dark, heavy clothes. He had a black beard, a black cap, and bright, black eyes. He continuously smiled as he answered questions.

"Ya. Ya. Tito's," he said pointing to himself and the other rebels.

This confirmed what the Americans had thought; these were the Partisans of Tito. The man told them that they were trying to take them to a place where they could be airlifted back to their base. He said that there was a long way to go before reaching what he called the "Valley of Freedom."

"I lived in America," he proclaimed proudly. "In Michigan"

"Michigan? I am from Michigan," Stoney said.

"What is your name?" he asked. He was the first rebel to ask anyone their names.

"Stoney, Bill Stoney - what is yours?"

"I name Goran."

Goran had lived in Michigan in the early twenties. He worked in the steel mills, and while he was there he got into a barroom fight and accidentally killed a man. He ran away from the law and did not stop running until he reached the mountains of Yugoslavia. He looked at Stoney's feet and said, "I find boots for you." A while later he came back holding a pair of military, nail-studded mountain climbing boots and a pair of thick khaki socks. Stoney felt as though it was Christmas and he had gotten the gift he had always wanted. Smiling, he slipped the socks and boots on his feet. They were a bit tight but far better than walking barefoot.

"Thank you," he exclaimed, pumping his hand in gratitude.

"Okay friend, good, good," he assured him while tapping on Stoney's shoulder.

"You leave soon," he said and explained that they had to cross the next valley that night.

He told the Americans that, in the valley, there was a German-held town they had to pass undetected. "Will be dark, Germans not see you," Goran said. "Must be very quiet, like mice," he smiled as he walked his fingers through the air between the Americans.

Soon after, the Americans were ordered to move out. Goran waved to them as he left, and they all wished he was going with them. Soon the village was far behind as the team worked their way down to the valley. Apparently, they had to cross this valley to get to the next relatively safe mountain range. They moved along quietly. One of the Partisans walked some distance ahead of the team, scouting the territory.

They were almost at the foot of the mountain when the scout came back carrying a flashlight wrapped in a cloth to dim the light. The rebels gathered around and began to talk, several of them making hand gestures in different directions. This was new. The Partisans didn't talk much unless there was a problem to solve.

They signaled for the Americans to move on, parallel to the mountains, toward the town. They all forged forward along the trail, in the dim light of a quarter moon. Eventually, they could see the road, a road that they had to cross, and now they could understand the problem. A large convoy of German trucks was growing along the road using only blackout lights. The trucks were probably carrying ammunition, food, medical supplies and, possibly, army troops. They were running in blackout for their protection.

The Americans made their way down to within a few yards of the road. There, they were motioned to sit down and wait. The convoy was moving very slowly and finally came to a halt. The fainted images of the trucks were illuminated by their slight blackout lights. Soon men jumped out of the cabs. Most headed off toward the rear of the convoy where the ration trucks were. About a half dozen stayed behind and spread out to guard the convoy.

With hand gestures, the rebels made everyone understand they were to run across the road near the trucks, one man at a time, and reunite on the other side several yards away from the road. It was about twenty-five yards to get from one side of the road to the other. Two of the rebels ran across the road, then three of the crewmen followed, one by one. Another rebel rose with his arm around Ryker's waist to help support him while crossing. Ryker half-ran and was half-pulled to the other side.

Chris Moody saw their shadows disappear into the darkness on the other side of the road; he sighed in relief. One of the remaining rebels tapped Moody on the shoulder signifying that it was his turn to run. He ran downward a few feet from the trucks. The shoulder of the road fell away sharply under his feet, and his right foot caught on an ironwood bush. Chris jerked his leg while still running. A ripping sensation and a searing pain tore through the right side of his groin. His foot came free, but when he tried to put weight on it, Chris felt excruciating pain. His right leg crumpled under him and he fell hard on his back. Chris Moody saw stars in the now overcast sky. He rolled over onto his stomach and looked around anxiously to see if he had attracted any attention.

The Germans still had their guns slung casually on their shoulders. With a quiet groan, Chris rose to his feet and stumbled towards the road, half dragging his right leg. Finally, he reached the other side and stumbled down a shallow embankment into the arms of Manny Cardenas. Then he collapsed in agony as everyone waited in tense silence for the rest of the crew and rebels to make it across the road. When they all gathered again, the silent command was to move out. Moody clenched his teeth against the extreme pain and limped forward. The next town was dark and wrapped in silence; a blackout to prevent Allied bombers from seeing it. The moon was hiding behind the clouds. The running team formed a single file line, holding on to the shirt of the person ahead of them to avoid getting lost in the pitch-black night. Moody's head and groin ached. It was extremely difficult to walk.

The Partisan with the muffled flashlight led the way, and the rest of them followed, shuffling along like a giant caterpillar, crawling in and out between buildings and freezing when dogs barked. The flashlight appeared and disappeared as the leader turned corners. They were nearly out of town when a door opened, casting a dim beam of light into the night. A German officer swaggered out of the door, clutching the hand of a woman. Both were laughing, perhaps drunk. Everyone froze and dared not breathe. The dim light from the door, just across the street, seemed as bright as searchlight.

The door slammed shut and the man and woman walked unsteadily down the road, about twenty-five feet away. The running men's bodies pressed against the side of the building, and for one moment, whether due to intuition or a slight noise, the officer seemed to look intently in their direction, but he was soon distracted by the woman pulling his hand. She led him away, and the team disappeared into the night and out of town.

Once free from the town, someone cut a cane from an ironwood bush and handed it to Moody. The team came to a railroad track and followed for a mile to a bridge that crossed a river. On the other side of the river, the men sat and rested. Two of the rebels headed back down to the railroad track. The Americans were still catching their breath and sipping their rationed water when several explosions rocked in the silence of the night.

The two rebels were running back, the rest of the rebels jumped to their feet and urged all to rush up the mountainside as sirens howled behind them. Apparently, the rebels had blown up the railroad bridge and it was still ablaze with their handiwork. The sky was flooded with light as the Germans searched the skies for aircraft. When none were found, the anti-aircraft floodlights turned to the hillside where the running men were making their way upwards. The rebels were light-footed and confident as they climbed the mountain face. The Americans followed the best they could as the searchlights closed in on them.

Moody closed his eyes against the sharp pain in his thigh and groin. There were sounds of men breathing hard surrounding him while climbing, and searchlights bearing down on them.

"Sakrij se!" (Hide!) yelled their leader.

Even those who didn't speak the language knew he was telling them to hide. Everyone jumped behind boulders and trees and froze, just as the giant swath of light washed over them. As soon as it passed by, they ran again, flying along the hillside while searching lights were chasing them. As the runners angled their course upward, some were blinded by the lights and stumbled, catching themselves with their hands against the ground. After several hundred yards the lights were circling back.

"Sakrij se!"

Once again, they all ducked and held still. The lights briefly illuminated the hillside; the brightness was in stark contrast to the deep night darkness. The runners felt vulnerable as they were exposed to their hunters. The lights passed on, searching the mountain repeatedly. But the hunted men kept running, frequently looking back over their shoulders.

In this manner, fleeing in the dark, they made their way up the forest and away from the searching lights They were now into the mountainside's thick forest and away from the valley. They dodged the ever-sweeping beams until the searchlights could no longer reach them. Then, they ran another half mile just to be safe. The team went over a low ridge, and up to the far side of another ridge, high up on the mountain, and then the group collapsed on the ground. The rebels were not particular out of breath, but they seemed relieved and the Americans hoped that this meant they were out of danger for the moment.

"I can't believe they blew that bridge with us sitting right there!" Ryker gasped in astonishment

"Man, I wish I could run faster if they are going to pull

stunts like that," Stoney said.

Moody was lying on the ground breathing hard, eyes closed, facing up to the sky. The rebels took a small drink of water and signaled for the rest to do the same. They all rested for a few minutes more and then began walking, still heading up the side of the mountain.

Trails of Tragedy and Triumph

6

TURBULENCE

John Mueller was taken away by strangers who were roaming up in the mountains. He did not know where he was going and, he was uncertain of how long he would be following them. It was like his childhood when he was lost in the mysterious and strange world of grown-up people. The rebels surrounding him did not even know his name; they did not ask. They just kept on walking, taking him wherever they wished.

As a child, growing up in Freeport, Michigan, he was helpless at the mercy of his parent who seemed unable to make up their minds. When his mom and dad were together, they were miserable and when apart, they hated one another. John Mueller, as a child, never had a place to call home. He moved constantly.

Mueller would have never thought that years later, he would have similar feelings of helplessness. That once again his fate would be in the hands of people dragging him along. However, he understood that this was different. Mueller felt a strange bonding with these rugged people with whom he had very little in common. Their ideology, religion, culture, lifestyle, could not be any further apart, yet, Mueller felt this overwhelming security and genuine admiration for these people who were risking their lives to save his.

Like most people, John Mueller could not recollect his

very early years. He did not remember being held, happy, hungry or crying. His memories seem to begin at five when he started first grade and met his best friend, Bill Stoney. One day, a year later, John's mother told him that he did not have to go to school. His little heart raced with the idea of spending the day outside rolling his beat-up train, through the sand. He would be out with his friend, playing with the neighbors' dog or playing a game of stick toss.

His mother was hanging laundry. His father had gone to work at the Cotton Mill. Yes, this was going to be a great day. The neighbor, a man named Henry came to visit, driving his shiny black open touring car with side curtains. That was nothing unusual. Henry came over often to visit. He drove past little John and pulled all the way into their garage. Henry, his wife, and daughter had been close friends with the Mueller family for some time. John did not think anything out of the ordinary was happening when Henry and his mother began to pack some of their belongings and put them in the backseat of his car.

"Are we going for a ride, Mother?" John asked.

"Yes, John," she replied. "We are going for a short trip."

Mother seemed tense as she forced a cheerful expression to keep John from asking too many questions.

"But I want to stay home and play," the boy begged.

She did not answer him. She was busy throwing clothes and belongings into the back seat of Henry's car. Then she tossed John on top of all the clothes in the backseat, and they drove west, leaving behind a cloud of dust.

John looked out the back window of the car. His train lay motionless on the sand. Jack, his dog also lay in their yard, his head resting on his paws. His sad brown eyes watched the car until it was out of sight. John turned from the back window and snuggled down into the clothes piled high in the backseat of the car, thinking of his friend Bill.

The rain had begun to fall and as they drove the storm intensified. John closed his eyes against the lightning, the thunder and the powerful rain that was now beating against the car.

"Mom, please, let's go home," he pleaded once more.

"Our home is ahead of us son," she replied.

Finally, the car stopped at a roadside park by the muddy banks of a river. Henry pitched a tent, but the feeling was not that of a fun camping adventure. Little John's mood was as damp and uncomfortable as Henry's tent. The sun set, and they spent the night crowded together in the tent. John missed his bed, his warm room and he missed his friend Bill and, he was wondered what his dad was thinking about now.

Henry left in the morning to go to work in the city; he was a motorcycle policeman. When he returned in the late afternoon, he and mother spent a lot of time together, walking, laughing, and holding each other. They had little time for John. Henry seldom looked at John let alone spoke to him. For several weeks, John did not go to school. He spent his time playing by the river. Eventually, his mom entered him into a school about a half mile away. When John asked her when he would be seeing his dad and his friend Bill again, his mother would answer,

"We will see them sometime." Little did he knew that she was hiding from his dad.

One day when John got home, his mother wasn't there. Henry did not usually get back to the tent until dinnertime. It was still hours before nightfall, yet the day had gone dark. Thick, threatening clouds covered the sky. The wind was blowing, lifting leaves from the ground and twisting them in the air. John sat in the tent door, his arms wrapped around his legs, and his head rested on his knees.

As the storm intensified, the wind gathered force and began to bend the branches of trees. Heavy rain pounded on the ground. Thunder boomed, and lightning splintered the air. He crawled inside the tent, zipped it up and hid in his sleeping bag. He lay there for some time as the wind whistled and howled, shaking the tent like a rag. The storm had broken loose and driving rain slashed down on the tent. In the midst of the pandemonium of terrible sounds, he heard nearby trees falling. He curled up and closed his eyes and waited to be carried off in the gale. He finally fell into a fitful sleep and dreamed of roaring trains, flashing lights, and wailing mothers.

Little John suddenly awoke, he was relieved to see the tent was still standing and that he was safely in it. He cautiously crawled out of his sleeping bag, unzipped the front door, and went out. The river was swollen, transformed from a sleepy, green flow to a loud, brown torrent. Fallen trees and debris littered the river bank. When mother and Frank came home, John hardly noticed them.

The next day, he found a fishing line in the old toolbox. Searching the tent, he found a safety pin behind a pile of papers and he twisted it into a hook. He dug some worms from the muddy banks of the river, placed them in an old milk can, and began what was to be his favorite pastime.

7

FRIENDS FOR LIFE

After a couple of hours heading upwards in the mountain, the running team stopped in a circular clearing between thick tree trunks. The canopy of tall trees created a natural roof to protect them from any danger coming from the air. The night was cloudy and cold, and the group was so weary with physical exertion and mental strain that sleep came quickly to everyone. For the injured Chris Moody, the climb has been excruciating. Spasms of pain racked his body radiating from his groin, where the pain was concentrated, to his limbs and guts. The ache even made its way to his eyes and head. Every time he stepped on an uneven surface, a charge orbited through his body.

Andy Ryker also had a difficulty keeping up since his ankles were still swollen. Behind this peripatetic group, there were sounds of alarms, searchlights weaving in the darkness, and voices yelling in the distance. The havoc that had followed the explosion was still deafening and the shadows of the Germans still haunted them. The Americans followed the light-footed rebels, running away from danger, to darkness and possibly to safety. Moody had no choice but to move on and endure the pain.

Along the way, he clenched his teeth, planted his cane on the ground, and lifted himself up, keeping up with the relentless pace of the rebels.

Mueller and Stoney lay next to each other, looking at the tree canopy, reminiscent the past. They've been friends since they were small children when the lived a couple of houses apart. Even after Bill Stoney got married and John Mueller was engaged, their homes were in the same neighborhood. Now as night had fallen, and John Mueller lay on the cold, hard ground, he thought back to his childhood. Then, it had been mother and Frank who occasionally glanced back to see if he was following, not noticing his emotional state. He knew pain then, too. He was a child living in confusion, always on the move, running from the past and moving on to a dark and uncertain future. After his parents divorced, his mother and Frank moved into an awful cement blockhouse. His father was allowed to come and see him and take him away some weekends. Those weekends were the happiest moments of his young life. For a few days, his heart would replenish with the joy and security that his father's presence afforded.

Bill Stoney's parents stayed together till the end. Little John spent a lot of time in his friend's home, where he found security and food. The two boys grew up during the great depression and times were difficult for everyone. Bill Stoney faced death before, as a child. His grandma Lou loved to go for an occasional ride with their Model-T Ford. His Father always volunteered to take grandma for a ride and this one Sunday dad asked Bill to come along. Little Bill was wearing a new overcoat, one that his mom had made for him. He was proud of the new overcoat; it made him feel special.

Anticipating the ride and the time he would spend with his dad, he jumped for joy. But, his joy wore out a bit when he had to sit in the passenger's seat with grandma. Little Bill loved his grandma, but the idea that he would have to share the seat with her three-hundred pounds was a tormenting thought. Grandma's lap became Bill's seat. His head was pressed against the ceiling since her large body left little room for the boy.

Shortly after his dad drove away from the house, sprinkles of rain began to fall from the sky. Bill was very happy, despite the discomfort of sharing a seat with grandma. He watched his dad with pride and admiration, as he drove his new car. Father turned to look at Bill and smiled once and a while.

"Watch the road," grandma ordered with her authoritarian voice. Father minded until he knew she was not watching, then he turned and winked at his son, and they both smile. The rain was now coming down hard and it was difficult to see the road ahead. Father was driving with one hand because he used his other hand to operate the manual windshield wiper. They were going to visit dad's brother in his new home. The downpour continued, and they tried in vain to read the cross-street signs obscured by the rain. They were looking for a street named Vernon. As the search continued, Bill was getting tired and he was cold. Squeezed between his grandmother and the hard car top, he was increasingly uncomfortable. Grandma's labored breath blew across his face and he was nauseated with the smell of stale beer.

Please, please, Bill begged in silence, let them find Vernon Street. He just about had enough of this ride.

"There," yelled grandma, "there is Vernon." She pointed to the right.

Father was looking to the left. He reacted quickly, instinctively turning the car to the right. Suddenly, the car broke over a little knoll, swung to the left, to the right, and to the left again. Then it began to skid on the wet street.

"Watch out! Watch out!" Bill heard the terror in grandma's blaring voice.

Directly in front of the car, there was a high concrete abutment where the road dead-ended. They were probably traveling at about thirty miles an hour when they hit the abutment straight on. The car came to an abrupt halt. Sounds of shattering of glass disturbed the quiet neighborhood.

Waves of flesh and fat from grandma's body propelled little Bill through the windshield. His little body rolled over the hood and fender and onto the muddy street. He felt the rain pouring hard onto his body. And, then darkness. He was blinded by the blood flowing into his eyes from the deep cuts above each of his eyebrows. He desperately tried wiping it away.

His father rushed to pick him up. "Are you okay, son?"

Other cars had stopped to help. Someone picked up the injured boy and put him in the back seat of their brand new Buick and rushed him to the hospital. Blood spattered onto the clean seat of the car. Bill's Father was trying to stop the bleeding with his handkerchief. Between his half-closed eyelids, he observed his dad's worrying face.

"I am okay dad," he said reassuringly.

Through the ripped shirt, Bill could see the black and blue imprint of the steering wheel on his dad's chest.

"We are almost to the hospital," said the kind voice of the man driving the car.

Grandma was not with them. Bill did not mind; he now had room to breathe. Grandma was spared without a scratch. Apparently, her body had enough natural padding to protect her.

Later in life, Bill always associated grandma with the invention of the airbags.

"You are fortunate to have hit the abutment. It prevented you from dropping six hundred feet over the hill," the driver told them, pointing at the slope of the hill.

After the boy was treated in the hospital, his dad was not able to fix his car and they took a taxi to his brother's house. Little Bill was heartbroken because his new, beautiful overcoat was torn and bloodstained beyond repair.

When they return home, his mother was mad. She gave father an earful. Dad listened without saying anything. In the end, he apologized. He said he knew that she was terrified at that thought of losing both of them.

"No Mom, I am okay. It wasn't dad's fault." Bill said.

"We'll see," she said.

Little Bill looked back over his shoulder and winked at his dad. They both smiled, knowing that mother would eventually soften up.

An eerie feeling overcame Bill Stoney as he lay atop of the mountain, resting before another day's walk. The voices of the Germans remained faded echoes. The searchlights had been replaced by darkness. The moon bashfully pulled over the clouds, enough to see the outline of the men beside him, some in a deep sleep, others restless. Stoney has always been a dreamer. It was the reason he enlisted – to save the world. It was serendipitous that after recruiting together with his best friend, John Mueller, and then training in separate training grounds, they finally ended up in the same base, a unit halfway around the world.

Bill Stoney felt the chill of the night in his legs. This was going to be another night among the ghosts of the past, one trying to foresee the images of the future. It was hours past midnight. Melancholy overcame his heart.

"What is this all about?" he wondered.

Humans were running like hunted animals, killing one another, and for what? In the name of peace, democracy, freedom - For what?

The howl of a wolf sounded off over the horizon. Stoney had to block out the aching of his body and the bitter cold to get some badly needed sleep. The morning would be here shortly, and the marathon walk would continue once again. He closed his eyes, dreaming of his warm, brand new overcoat that mother once made for him.

8

LOST

Chris Moody was exhausted, but each time he drifted off, sharp pain in his groin and leg wakened him. His body felt as though it was riddled with needles, and though he could keep his eyes open, the eyelids felt thick and weighted with fatigue - deep sleep continued to elude him.

"Please, God, let me rest for just a moment or two."

The sky was profoundly dark, and the night air was bitter cold and very still - not a breath of air was moving. He could hear men snoring. All around the clearing the men were curled into tight balls against the cold.

John Mueller was sleeping next to Bill Stoney mumbling in his sleep; he spoke of food, fishing, and telephones, only God knows what he was dreaming about. Moody smiled anyway, John had told him that his two favorite things were food and fishing. Moody drifted between exhaustion and twilight sleep. There were visions of warm sun, beaches crowded with vacationing families, a restaurant with linen-covered tables, sitting next to a beautiful woman. There were luxurious, rich foods, clean, tiled showers with fresh-smelling soap and dry fluffy towels, soft feather beds with crisp, cool sheets, and slippers nearby.

Moody tried to sleep, but each time he moved, even

slightly, searing pain blazed across his nerves. Groans did not escape him, but only because he bit his lip bloody. The sky to the east turned ash gray. Soon the rays of sunlight would fan up into the sky from the mountaintop. The men around him began to move. As they were waking up there were slight, unconscious grunts, stretched out legs and arms thrown over faces. Everyone was slow to stand up – thinking of the day ahead.

The rebels were already up, geared up to go, nudging everyone to get up and get going. Andy Ryker blinked his eyes, stared up at the sky for a moment, and then turned to look at Moody. His face registered concern.

"Chris, are you okay?" John asked.

"I am okay. I just want to get moving."

"Me too. Let's do it. Did you get any sleep?"

Chris Moody smiled and grimaced as the pain shot through his body once more. The sky was now blazing red, and the fiery edge of the sun was burning over the lines of mountain peaks to their left. As beams of light punctured the shadow of their protected hollow, the group left behind the drowsy voices, irritable exclamations, and yawns, ready to begin another Odyssey day. Chris Moody pulled himself up leaned on his cane and grasped a tree trunk. Andy Ryker leaned heavily against a tree for support. They looked at each other, shook their heads and smiled grimly.

"Well, we're quite a mess, aren't we?" Ryker said.

Then, Chris Moody borrowed a knife from one of the rebels and cut a few rings around the top of his cane. He was gingerly trying to put his weight on his right leg when Pastorelli came over to him.

"Come on, Chris, I'll help you walk."

Bob Pastorelli, their navigator, was of a medium size man,

lean and strong. Even though he was a Lieutenant, he treated all enlisted men as equals; he was well liked and respected.

"Thanks, Bob, but I think I can make it." Moody used his hand to move his right leg forward, then leaped on his left leg. Push, hop, push, hop, he made his way.

Pastorelli looked after Moody doubtfully but Moody did not want to slow anyone down and declined help from anyone. As the day wore on, he was able to put a little more weight on his right leg and could take a step without using his hand to help move his injured leg forward. He was flushed and sweating profusely despite the cool temperature of the day. Every little rock or pebble in his path caused nearly unbearable pain if his foot hit it, but somehow, he kept pace with the rest of the team.

The men of the running team stopped to rest every few hours and, especially Moody and Ryker, welcomed the chance to catch their breath. They worked their way down the backside of the mountain, still heading south, and then traveled through a small valley.

In the valley, greenery had pierced the earth, newly warm with thin spring sunshine. There were tender grass shoots, poppies, and wild daisies. By the time they were halfway to the next mountain, the sun was setting. Moody and Ryker followed the team; they kept putting one foot in front of the other, with dogged determination. The miles slipped by, every step they took they were a bit closer to freedom, a bit closer to home. All men were weak and dizzy from hunger and their clothes fit more loosely than they had just a few days ago, but their feet kept moving. Slowly home drew nearer - inches at a time. They could not and would not give up. Moody was hardly aware when their guides called for a halt. It was dark. His body buckled under the weight of weariness. He fell to his hands and knees, head hanging between his arms, then he rolled slowly over on his back. He closed his eyes and knew no more. Water splashed on his face and opened his eyes, startled. Surely, he was dreaming.

But there it was again – splat, splat, splat – coming a little faster now. There were fuzzy thoughts, but Moody finally realized that a light rain was falling. He sat up. The rest of the group was also rising. The rain soon became a downpour. The entire team moved towards a rock outcropping with the rebels urging the Americans on. In the heavy rain, they could see very little: vague shapes and occasional voices surrounded them.

"Stay close! Don't get lost," someone said.

Moody moved toward the voice. It was Ryker. He was close behind one of the rebels. They held on each other's hand to get through the muddy earth.

"Everyone, move to the rocks," voices were heard through the falling rain.

The earth was muddy, and Moody struggled to keep up. He followed the sounds of boots slapping and squishing up the hill. "Over here! Over here!"

Moody and Ryker moved toward the voices and found the rest of the crew of Lucky Lady huddled against the slightly overhung boulder.

"*Dodi ovamo!*" (Come here!) voices were calling from a little farther up the hill.

They went toward the voice and found the rebels in a large hollowed out area making a small cave-like space. Everyone squeezed under it and had a headcount. No one was missing. Beyond their shelter, in the darkness, the rain was falling hard. A melancholic feeling soaked through most of them as they stood dripping in a hollow cave, under the eerie sound of the raindrops, whipping in front of them and beyond the dense darkness. There was no lightning, no thunder, no anxiety for a moment or two, their minds were transfixed with the pressing force of the powerful downpour.

The rebels had congregated in the corner of the cave to share and preserve what warmth they could. The Americans did the same. There were teeth chattering and bodies shivering in the night chill. Bodies slumped against the rock, men against each other, listening to the rain which kept pounding on the earth harder and harder. Some men closed their eyes and then fell asleep. When they woke, the world was silent. The rain had stopped, and they began to move out again, heading up steep slopes now slippery with mud. They reached the mountaintop in the early hours of the morning, moved downwards on the other side, and came upon a small village.

It was a tiny gathering of perhaps a dozen small homes clinging to the side of the mountain. There were a few horses. Miraculously they managed to keep them from the Germans. The Germans were ruthless and thorough in their looting, making sure there was nothing left in the villages besides empty houses and hungry people. But the villagers were unconquerable. They could not be intimidated and continued to support the rebels with their little they had. The Americans were separated and directed inside the various homes of the villagers.

The rooms they entered were bare of furniture. In the center of the space was a large, flat stove, with wood burning on its top. The open fire made the room feel warm and welcoming. The men sat on the dirt floors, their feet towards the stove and fell asleep. The sounds of footsteps awoke Mueller and Stoney. An elderly woman dressed in a black dress and a black kerchief covering her head came into the room from outside. She walked towards the fire and they watched through half-opened eyelids. The room was dark, the only source of light was the slow-burning fire. The woman pushed at the fire with a pair of tongs, moving it toward the center of the stove block. She then wiped the surface of the block with a cloth. She reached into the pocket of her waist apron and pulled something out. The two men glimpsed two white oval objects. She held them between her fingers and with a quick move smacked each one against the side of the stove and lifted her hand above the hot surface. A stream of clear and yellow liquid fell to the stove-top. They heard sizzling. Their eyes were wide open now. Their stomachs rumbled, and their mouths watered. The elderly woman scooped the eggs with a spatula and slid it onto two plates. She turned and walked toward the two men, her arm extended, offering them the plates; on each plate was the most beautiful fried eggs they had ever seen and a healthy portion of polenta.

Their eyes must have glowed with delight because she chuckled and said, "*Jedi*." (Eat.) Her eyes were deep, dark, and kind. Her face was wrinkled and mystifying.

"*Jedi*," she repeated, handing them a spoon.

They took the plate. Her smile was toothless and affable. She walked to the door and the two men were overcome with guilt as they looked at the lovely egg, polenta and the beat-up tin plate. It was very likely that this woman was going without food herself to feed them.

The door closed behind her and their hunger overcame their guilt. They cut into the egg with the spoon and closed their eyes as the first bite of egg hit their tongue. They chewed slowly, relishing the flavor and texture. Then they took a bite of polenta and another of the egg. As they ate, a warm sensation grew in their body. Mueller's eyes closed again, and he imagined himself in a room full of tables laden with salads, fresh cheeses, and hot bread. A hand was holding a silver platter in front of his face and on it a giant, perfect egg. "*Jedi, Jedi,*" a voice said to him.

"*Moramo ici!*" (we must go!)

A rebel was standing in the doorway. Mueller opened his eyes, took his last bite, and stood up. The two men followed the rebel out the door. They went to the center of the village where there was a small square and a hand-operated water pump. The rest of the rebels and the crew of Lucky Lady were there. They all washed their faces and shaved with razors provided by the villagers. With a content stomach and a fresh shave, they followed the group down the mountain trail with a feeling of renewed vigor.

Trails of Tragedy and Triumph

9

THE CALENDAR

Even though the Americans had a renewed energy after washing and shaving, they remained silent as they trekked down the mountain. Far below, in the valley, the beauty of a yellow and red blanketed earth unfolded before them. It extended into deep greenery on the far mountain slopes. Suddenly a melodic voice disrupted the gloomy silence. The low singing voice increased to a loud but restrained sound. The beautiful melody made everyone look at Manny Cardenas, "*Ay, ay, ay, ay, Canta y no llores, Porque cantando se alegran, Cielito lindo los corazones...*"

"That is beautiful," Chris Moody mumbled as the voice continued to soothe the ears of the weary airmen. Then he turned to Clark Bailey and asked, "Do you understand the words?"

"I am not fluent in Spanish, but I believe he is saying; "Sing and don't cry, because singing cheers up, pretty little darling."

Manny Cardenas, six feet tall, tanned with thick black hair, looked at his friends, smiled and with an animated voice said, "*Amigos, todos deben tener esperanza.*" (Friends, we all must have hope.)" And continued his singing.

A smile erased the gloominess from some faces.

"When did you learn to sing like this?" Clark Bailey asked Manny Cardenas.

"Well, my friend, I was born in Guadalajara, Mexico." and

he went on to explain about his father who was a great singer. His mother died when he was young and his father decided to marry an American girl of Mexican descent and move to El Paso Texas.

The aftermath of foreign domination, dictatorship, political revolution and a civil war that ended on 1920, left Mexico with dreadful infrastructure, minimal tourism, and political confrontations which contributed to a chaotic social landscape. This prepared the rising of the Mexican Renaissance. During the late thirties, there were signs of a revival of the Mexican cultural life which turned into a blossoming lifestyle in the early fifties. The unity of the Mexican people became synonymous with the cultural revolution by the artists. Cultural influences and behavior changed as people gathered at various events and clustered in small groups, chatting and conversing with one another. Art created a sense of purpose and began to beautify the public spaces by providing venues for collective expression.

The Mexican Revolution interrupted tourism in Mexico, but by the nineteen-thirties, things began turning around. Despite the Great Depression, there was an increase in American tourism to Mexico in the mid-thirties. The Mexican government, to attract tourists from around the world, began the development of beach resorts and the construction of upscale hotels in several major cities. Guadalajara was famous for some of Mexico's best-known traditions, such as mariachi music and it became the epicenter of Mexican arts. The city was also known as a pioneer in the underground arts scene and attracted wealthy artists who wanted to live the Bohemian lifestyle. The city's diversity of western European architectural styles mixed with Mexican cultural structures made Guadalajara very attractive to tourists, especially to cultural tourism.

Mexicans value family hierarchy and parents are treated with a high level of respect. The families are usually large and there is a strong connection between family members, which includes extended family and close friends. Manny's mother passed when he was too young to remember, and he was raised by his father and his aunts. In the early nineteen-thirties, Manny's father assembled a singing trio and performed in cantinas, in parks and various events. Manny, followed his father everywhere and sometimes the little boy sang along. It was a good tourist attraction to see an adorable boy with an angelic voice singing Mexican songs. It was at one of those events that Manny's dad met Carmen. The two fell in love, they got married and moved to El Paso. Manny was nine-years-old, and Carmen was the only mother he knew.

"America has been good to me. At some point, I wanted to serve and to protect America from enemy threats. It is a great honor." He told Clark Bailey.

"What about your dad?" Bailey asked.

"My dad and my mom are still in El Paso. He still likes to sing, and my mom is a great cook. I can't wait to go back and eat some of her pozole soup and her delicious enchiladas."

"I like enchiladas," Bailey reacted. Cardenas was quick to correct Bailey's pronunciation of the word. After spending several minutes to teach Bailey how to roll his tongue and pronounce a few Spanish words correctly, he gave up.

"But you are still invited for my mom's cooking when we are back in the states." he said.

Bailey, who was easily spotted within the group because of his golden blond hair, tall and graceful demeanor, smiled on the thought of homemade foods. The running team walked until sundown. They found a small barn at the far end of the picturesque valley and made it their home for a few hours. The men of the group slept laying on the thick layers of hay. Chris Moody's sleep was restless again even though he was exhausted from walking most of the previous day. Rays of sun shone through the cracks of the old barn, highlighting bits of hay and dust floating around. Cautiously, Moody sat up and tested his stiff, sore right leg. He picked up his cane and carved another ring on its tip, keeping track of their days on the run. He thought back and tried to remember how many days had passed before he began to carve the rings on his cane. His life had become a walking dream of disjointed events, his feet plodding up a mountain, his hands reaching for a taste of polenta, his eyes scanning the horizon for enemies. He had never dreamed he could survive in such circumstances. Moody was a news buff. It was a tormenting feeling being isolated from the world and not knowing the latest news or how the war was progressing. He did not deal well with the unknown - Where would the end of the day find him? On what ground would he find himself lying for a rest? Chris Moody was physically prepared for long distance hiking. He grew up in Northern Arizona where the mountain hiking trails are long and challenging. He was also a skilled skier - his favorite sport. However, he never imagined hiking trails of this magnitude.

He glanced at the human figures in the dim barn, to him, people reduced to hunted animals, sleeping on frozen grounds, longing for a bite of food was like animals do in a barren land - this was the ultimate human tragedy. The American survivors spent every minute of the day and the night together, but there was a minimal exchange of words between them. Everyone was preoccupied with the uncertainty of the future. Yet, they all believed that they would come out of this adventure alive. George Poulos was the first one to get up. Moody did not know him very well, he had been new to their crew. George was their co-pilot and he seemed very friendly, polite, and efficient. He wore his flight suit and sheep-lined boots the entire time. He came and sat beside Moody.

"How are you feeling, Chris?"

"My leg feels a little better."

George Poulos pulled a photograph from his breast pocket. It was a photograph of a group of people, varying in age, from very old to very young. "This is my Greek family," he said and began to explain everyone's name and relation. Chris Moody responded by saying that he was engaged to a wonderful girl and he too someday wanted to have a big family.

Moody remembered a couple of days ago when Bill Stoney showed him a photograph with his fiancé and their little boy; the woman was standing slightly behind the boy, who looked about two years old. Both had a bright smile and seemed happy.

"The love of my life and our son," Stoney had said. "They're back in Michigan." After a moment of silence, he continued, "I would like to play catch with my son someday."

"You will, Bill. We are going to get through this."

"I hope so," he replied as he placed the picture back in his pocket, a tear rolled down his cheek. This was the first emotion Chris Moody had witnessed from any of the crew members. A little humanity entered his heart; a tenderness that was forgotten in this inhumane race for survival.

As the rest of the group rose and prepared for another marathon walk, Bill Stoney wondered if everyone was as hungry as he was. They had not eaten since the previous morning when he had his egg and polenta. He stood up as well. The boots he had been given were holding up well. They had become more pliable and felt comfortable on his feet. The men seldom took their boots off; they had to be ready to run at any moment. While Stoney was testing his boots, he realized his flight suit felt particularly itchy. He had the sensation of small pieces of straw falling on his chest. He took off the top piece and shook it out. No straws there. Then he saw little red bumps on his skin. Bites! Quickly, he searched his jacket and found the culprits; Lice. Stoney stripped off his cut-off pants and socks in haste and noticed other men in the barn were doing the same. All over the room, men were jumping up, flinging off clothes, and examining their itchy hides.

"Just what we need, Lice!" someone exclaimed. There was a general chorus of grunts in agreement as they tried to pick their clothes clean of the little infesters.

Andy Ryker looked over at John Mueller, and said, "The lice are having a three-legged race on John's back!"

"They are also racing on places that I don't want to discuss," John answered.

Everyone laughed, even the rebels, who seemed to have somehow avoided the scourge. And had backed into a corner of the barn to avoid any close contact with the Americans, and their itchy visitors. In a few minutes, when they've done their best to clean their bodies and clothes, they again dressed and set out on the day's march, but there were frequent hushed exclamations and much slapping of bodies as more fleas came out of hiding. The rebels kept their distance and signaled the Americans to walk behind them. They were not taking any chances. They marched for hours, and in the afternoon, they came to a small valley. Ahead, a mountain towered steep and high. At the foot of the mountain lay a small village and there was a wide trail going up the mountain slope. The team headed toward the village and were welcomed by approximate forty people. This was a higher population than the previous villages. The inhabitants were all grown men and women. The people kindly offered them the omnipresent polenta and water, and an unusual treat, a small piece of ham for each of them. The Americans were moved by the generosity of the rebels and their supporters, sharing with them the little food that they had. When they finished their Spartan but much-appreciated meal, the rebels lead them through the village. Just past the village they came into an open space and saw, sitting on a narrow-gauge railroad track, an old railroad engine with several cars connected behind it. Some were open, gondola-style cars, and others were closed boxcars. The train track led from the village up to the side of the mountain. The American crewmen all looked at one another, not sure whether to be amused or afraid. The old steam engine looked very old and well worn! The rebels and more than a dozen villagers climbed onto the open cars and signaled for the Americans to board one of the other boxcars.

"*Nema usi!*" (No lice!) one of the rebels explained, pointing to their bodies and laughing.

The boxcar for Americans did not have doors, so they sat in the open doorways on each side of the car, their feet hanging out into space as the engine chugged laboriously up the mountain leaving below them the valley and brown-roof homes of the village. The sun was hot, but the breeze stirred their hair and cooled their skin as the train slowly climbed the slope. The Americans began to relax, enjoying the luxury of the ride. Some men closed their eyes, faces lifted to the sun and cool air. Some picked fleas off their clothes while their eyes took in the broad expanse of mountainsides embroidered with patches of green trees. Chris Moody watched the landscape through half-closed eyes. Andy Ryker was sitting next to him.

"Wouldn't it be nice if we could ride this a few hundred miles," Chris said.

Ryker stuck his head out the door, craning his neck to see the track ahead of them, then looked doubtful and chuckled, "We'll be lucky if it gets us to the top of the mountain."

Chris smiled in agreement. Their concern was also the frequent repair patches on railroad track running beneath their feet. After the Germans bombed out and damaged the track, the repairs looked makeshift and did not inspire confidence. Andy and Chris pulled their feet in and held onto the side of the car. They had been on the train for about a half hour, and they were nearly to the top of the mountain. The view was spectacular: mountains marched into the distance, range after range. Green valleys in the deep gorges dispersed with spring blossoms. Gracious trees covered the lower slopes in a green superior embrace. The men began to relax again under the amazing beauty of this land. The chug, chug, chugging of the train had lulled some of them into a dreamy state.

Suddenly, the sound of the train changed. Now it was laboring with great bellows and growls and was slowing down. The locomotive pulled, and the train gained a few yards. A blast of smoke and a roar from the engine, and it gained a few yards more, but still, it slowed. With a screech and a hiss, the engine gave a final, desperate tug, and then it stopped. For a moment, everyone stood still. The train stood motionless as well. Then the train began to inch backward, slowly at first, then faster.

"The engine's failed! Everyone hold on!" someone yelled.

The Americans lunged onto the corners of the boxcar, grasping for a handhold on the smooth, wooden walls. There was a loud squeal as the operator applied the train's brakes. The cars lurched to a stop and go as the brakes held and then let loose, held and let loose again. They were still going way too fast, and the thought of the makeshift track paralyzed Chris – along with the visions of the train rolling down the mountain smashing into pieces on the sharp rocks. His fingernails scraped along the walls as he tried to hold in place. The other men were also struggling to brace themselves against the floor and sides of the car, eyes wide open with concern, as the car continued to lurch, and the squealing of the brakes was joined with the smell of hot metal. Chris was slowly being jerked toward the door, his feet planted against the wooden floorboards, his arms dragging along the wooden wall. Every time the train lurched and slowed, he pushed himself toward the back of the car, and toward the door as the car swayed wildly back and forth. He was losing ground and feared that at any moment he would fly out of the boxcar and slam into the rocks along the tracks.

"Grab my hand!" It was Andy, stretching out his hand toward Chris, his other hand holding tightly to a metal knob of some sort on the wall.

Chris flipped on his stomach and stretched out his hand toward Andy. The train lurched, and Chris slid farther away. The train paused, and Chris lunged toward the extended hand. Again, the train lurched forward, again he fell flat on his stomach. Chris inched his way forward, hand outstretched, and just as his fingertips touched Andy's, the motion of the train smoothed out and slowed down. The operator had gained control of the sliding train. It was now easing much more slowly down the mountain.

Andy grasped Chris hand and pulled him into a sitting position next to him. They both sighed with relief as did the rest of the men, relaxed and sprawled on the boxcar floor.

"That would have been a hell of a way to go." Someone said with an agitated voice.

"I guess we should have packed parachutes." Another answered cheerfully.

Everyone laughed. But their laughter was short-lived as the roar of an airplane engine hit their ears. A nearby explosion deafened them. It came from the front of the train. A German fighter was now circling above the train and planning its attack. It had already dropped a bomb that had destroyed the railroad tracks in front of the train. The pilot made a broad turn and swept toward the train, coming in low, firing his guns. The bullets peppered the ground in a path leading up the train. The men on the train flung themselves down onto the floor, as bullets were striking the train. There was the sound of machine gun fire from one of the gondolas as the rebels shot at the attacker. The German fighter circled around and fired a few shots from the other side of the train and then flew away from the threat of ground fire. The train reached the bottom of the mountain and was gliding across the open space toward the village where they started.

"Hold on!" someone shouted.

The train came to an abruptly hold as it hit a pile of dirt at the end of the railroad tracks. As the men emptied the boxcar, jumping lightly to the ground. The faces of the rebels were full of fury as they ran up to the train operator, screaming and pointing alternately at the engine then the pile of firewood. Though the Americans could not understand their exact words, they figured out that the operator had failed to take along enough fuel to take the train to the top of the mountain.

Two of the villagers who were on the train had been shot in the fighter's attack; they had blood on their feet and arms. No one else was injured. One of the rebels pointed up to the tracks. There was a gap in the rail where the German fighter had damaged it. There would be no second try.

"*Mozemo ici ovuda!*" (We must go this way!) a rebel said. He was pointing to a vague trail on the side of the mountain. After a brief rest, the Americans followed the rebels up the trail toward the mountaintop.

"You know, suddenly, walking doesn't seem so bad," Andy Ryker said with a smile. The rest of them had to agree as they began their trudge up the mountain. The sun had become an enormous orange wheel as it sank into the west. Shortly after nightfall, the men stopped to rest.

Trails of Tragedy and Triumph

10

DAY OF JUDGMENT

Art Bauer was lying down on the ground to rest, thinking of how ironic it was that they did not gain an inch of land on the only ride they got on this entire journey, and that they had to walk an extra forty to forty-five minutes to get to the top. He reminisced back to his childhood when one of his chores was to search the railroad tracks and pick up small lumps of coal that had fallen from the trains.

Sometimes, he had to walk two to three miles down the tracks to collect just one pail of coal. The coal was used to fire up the old iron range his mother used to cook their meals. Having a little coal was crucial to survival.

Art Bauer grew up in the mining town of Davey, in West Virginia. His family was poor and barely kept up paying the rent. His father was a laborer, always looking for daily work but employment was difficult during the challenging days of the Great Depression. His grandparents had moved in with his family and, along with his two younger sisters, their little home was crowded. But that's what most people did those days. They stayed together to survive by any means.

Art and his two sisters amused themselves by filling pails of water and pouring them into gopher holes in order to drive them out. Despite their efforts, Art never saw a gopher coming out of a holes, even though there were hundreds of holes.

Lying on the ground, he thought about gophers and compared them with rebels up on the mountains. The rebels were everywhere, and the Germans had a difficult time trying to flush them out. Art was always fascinated by his grandmother. He would watch her make home brew beer and whiskey in twenty-gallon crocks.

"It is under my doctor's advice," she would say to him.

Art was doubtful that his grandmother was telling him the truth. But if the brew was good for her, let it be. It was apparently good for the other folks, so she sold it to them and it seemed to make everyone happy. Besides, grandmother helped with the home expenses. Art Bauer wet his lips with his tongue. A few swallows of that brew would make him happy right now.

He smiled as he remembered that one night carloads of police and revenue officers surrounded their neighborhood. Tough-looking men searched their house and found Grandmother's home brewing operation. The brewing crock was the first thing to go, busted into hundreds of pieces. Grandmother, a feisty woman, stood in the middle of the tough men screaming, "this brew is a prescription for my customers." She protested over and over. But the officers would not listen. They loaded the full bottles of brew into their cars.

Grandmother would not quit. She tried to convince the officers to call her doctor, to confirm what she was saying. The officers shrugged their shoulders and left, taking the full bottles of brew, not paying attention to his grandmother who was calling them thieves and thugs for taking her prescription brew. The doctor was apparently a man who took a real interest in the well-being of his patients because he visited quite often to sample his "prescription" and to ensure that it was just right for grandmother.

While grandmother made home brew and bootlegged it, some of her customers were buying uncut moonshine by the gallon. They used to mix the whiskey with water to yield more liqueur. Then they would sell it to their customers.

Art's grandmother was a piece of work. She had hidden a few gallons of whiskey in jugs in the weeds along the fence row about three hundred feet from the house. While the officers were searching the homes, they didn't look along the fence, so grandmother saved some of her whiskey. In a way, this was good news, because she would make enough money to pay the rent, so they could stay in the house a while longer. Shortly after this episode, Grandpa and Grandma, moved to a nearby city to start their liquor business there. Art Bauer was of short stature but solidly built. He was pretty good at boxing for his weight and was getting better, at a competitive level, before joining the Army Air Corps to serve his country. Being the smallest guy in school, he had to take boxing lessons from a young age to protect himself from the bullies. Art was relatively equally matched in speed, precision, agility, and style with the best. He won several amateur championships growing up until he made a gallant attempt to reach the finals of the National Collegiate Athletic Association Competition in the late thirties when he was a freshman at the University of Virginia

Without false modesty, Art would say that he was pretty good and, on every chance he got, he demonstrated his ability to shaft his shoulder into a right jab and lift up his right heel just before the strike. "That gives the jab more power and more leveraged weight than they have." he would say.

Art Bauer had bonded with Shaun O'Brien, an unlikely pair since Shaun was from Boston, tall, movie-handsome and much more modest than Art. Maybe it was grandma's whiskey business that connected those two. Shaun O'Brien was married shortly before the United States forces threw their power into World War II. His new wife, Dorothy, was from a wealthy and prominent family in Boston. Shaun was Irish, a descendant of a group of people who had come to Boston by the hundreds of thousands after the Great Famine in Ireland. Bostonians, considered the Irish to be ill-mannered, and uneducated. Consequently, if you were an Irish man in Boston in that period, you had to fight for respect. Shaun thought this kind of discrimination of the Irish in Boston was ironic since he was born in America. Upon arrival in Boston and, desperate for food and shelter, the Irish refugees took any unskilled jobs they could find such as cleaning yards and stables, unloading ships, pushing carts, and cleaning sewers. They immediately grabbed onto the lowest rung of society and waged a daily battle for survival as they clawed and climbed their way up the ladder called the "American Dream."

In Ireland, throughout the Famine years, between 1845 and 1855, one million people died and over a million emigrated to the United States.

Cultural and religious differences between the Irish Catholic refugees and Boston natives took over one-hundred years to be resolved. In their private time, after a hard day of work, Dorothy educated Shaun on how to get along in with the Boston natives. The exodus of European immigrants became a torrent of humanity in the late nineteenth and early twentieth centuries when millions of Europeans searched for a better opportunity elsewhere. Million migrated to the United States during that period. This migration downpour was several years after the widespread uprising across Europe, the so-called Liberal Revolution of 1848. A series of republican revolts against European monarchies, began in Sicily, and spread to several countries such as France, Germany, Italy, Greece and the Austrian Empire.

The struggling middle and working class, during the Liberal Revolution, attempted to establish new governments that allowed the common man a voice in government function. It failed to achieve any significant change in many countries. A great number of Europeans involved in the revolution, feared persecution for their actions during the uprisings, so they left their countries in search of a better political environment. The new wave of immigrants, years after the revolution, were laborers and poor, trying to find work in a new world where they were about to fight their biggest battle as they encountered the hostility of a new and unfamiliar society. In the United States they were the despised minority rooted in the working class and seemingly resistant to assimilation. This resulted in these Europeans suffering widespread discrimination in housing and employment. However, they couldn't look back since much of Europe couldn't support the rapidly growing population. Farmers struggled to make a living and factories were too few to provide jobs for everyone. Lack of grain drove up food prices while wages remained stagnant. With consumers buying less and less, profits plummeted, forcing thousands of industrial workers out of their jobs.

The revolutions of 1848 were expected to be a turning point in modern history, but modern history failed to turn and left behind a devastated society in a divided Europe. Most of the immigrants coming to the United States intended to stay for short periods, make some money and return home. A few of them did return to the homeland after making a bit of money, thinking that poverty was better than discrimination.

Some of the immigrants made the journey across the Atlantic with their family, while others travel alone, determined to work hard and to someday bring the rest of the family. Fathers were leaving their poor villages to work overseas; mothers were left alone to care for the children left behind, yearning for their fathers. Millions of European immigrants boarded steamships bound for the United States.

The journey was like nothing we see in the movies. There were no lovers sitting on the bow of the ship, watching it paring the blue waters, hair waving in the wind and dolphins swimming alongside. The poor travelers could only afford a ticket on steerage, a deck deep in the ship, below the quarter-deck.

They had to endure inhumane conditions; dreadful food, narrow beds in crowded compartments, no bathroom facilities, nowhere to bathe and unbearable stenches. They could take a walk on deck once a day and only in good weather, to breathe clean air. Once on the deck many of them had to be driven down; for they prefer the bitterness and danger of the storm to the degrading conditions below.

To forget their misery, they tried to amuse themselves by playing games, singing, and making music with accordions and mandolins. After almost two weeks, the travelers looked forward to stepping on solid grounds and breathing clean air. But every one of them knew full well that the biggest test was yet to come. All the suffering of leaving family and country behind, the endurance of that terrifying journey and the hope of a new life was all dependent on the immigration officers. Shortly after the ship dropped anchor, quarantine officers climbed aboard to check for signs of epidemic diseases.

If a ship was free of disease passengers were ferried to Ellis Island for inspection. They were jammed on a barge and as soon they arrived at Ellis Island and put the gangplank down, a man at the foot was shouted, "Drop your luggage here. Men this way. Women and children this way."

Families were separated, anticipating meeting back in the mound of luggage and hoping to find theirs. Thus, began the terrifying moments for most immigrants - this was the Day of Judgment. There were four to five hours of waiting for a brief medical examination, just a few seconds long.

Since most of the Europeans spoke no English and the doctors knew a handful of foreign words, part of the communication was done in sign language. At first, the doctors shined a light in their eyes and raised their eyelids with their fingers to check for inflammation on the inner eyelid. This would indicate if the person had the disease trachoma, a contagious eye infection, a common disease in southeastern Europe but relatively unknown in the United States.

After the eye exam the immigrants looked at the doctor with perplexed faces as they spoke, "Open your mouth" – "Lift your shirt" – "Cough" – "Again" words foreign to them. If a doctor found any indication of a disease which could have prevented them from earning a living, then the immigrant would be detained and possibly excluded from entering the United States. After the medical inspection there was a legal examination. Inspectors asked a series of fast questions, "Are you married or single?" - "What is your occupation?" "How much money do you have?" "Have you ever been convicted of a crime?"

The interrogation was over in a matter of minutes after which an immigrant was either permitted to enter the United

States or detained for a legal hearing. Again, the communication was difficult, and the process was so important since it determined the fate of a human being. Those who passed the medical examinations and the legal interrogation, now had to answer questions about how they planned to support themselves in the United States. People who did not pass these interrogation, could be sent home, even if other family members were allowed to enter. So many families were forced to separate that Europeans started calling Ellis Island - The Island of Tears.

Those who did not show enough money to survive had a second chance to call a relative living in the United States to vouch for him or her. The relative had to show money in the bank. Since they had no phone access and texting was about a century behind, the immigrant had to rely on a messenger to get a word - a lengthy process and more waiting in uncertainty. A detainee stay could last days or even weeks. Many were women and children who were waiting for a relative to come for them or for money to arrive. Others were waiting for a hearing in front of the board of special inquiry for a final decision. The program to enter the United States was exhausting for the officials and a nightmare for the immigrants but, at that time, it was the only way to handle that many people. The officers weren't unkind, just overloaded with tens of thousands of people entering the country. They were aware that the destiny of people's lives were in their hands, people full of fright, a few steps away from the new land or the return trip to the homeland. Ellis Island inspectors carefully weighed the prospects of new arrivals, especially those of women and children intending to rejoin husbands and fathers in this country. Those who survived the Day of Judgment, walked beyond the immigration station, on to a land of hope knowing there was a new life waiting for them. There were real opportunities, new customs, strange language, different holidays, even a different name for some of them since the spelling and the sounding were names that the English tongue cannot pronounce. Three of the Americans who were caught-up in the unimaginable adventure in Yugoslavia, while fighting for their country, were descendants of those who escape Europe's dark moments – Shaun O'Brien, Bob Pastorelli, and George Poulos.

Trails of Tragedy and Triumph

11

HIGHER AND HIGHER

There was an entire village on top of the mountain. Most of the buildings were in ruins, destroyed by German bombs, but a few homes still stood, etched on the sides of the mountain. They had survived the bombings because of their sheltered position.

There was an unusual amount of activity in the village, much more than the Americans had seen in previous communities. There were a few stores open, a general store with very little merchandise on display, a barbershop and a coffeehouse. There were other storefronts, but they were abandoned and most were in ruins. In the streets of this village, there was a rare mechanical mode of transportation. It was a strange looking invention, an automobile, like a Model T Ford, but it had a large upright boiler sitting on a platform sticking out of the rear of the car. The platform was loaded with wood. From time to time, the driver would get out and fill up the boiler with the wood. The vehicle could only go a few miles before it was time to throw in more wood. It was an ingenious innovation in response to German confiscation of gasoline.

The rebel guides stopped by the roadside coffee house. On the outside, under a huge platanus tree, there were a few round, iron tables and several wooden chairs with straw seats. On one of the chairs sat a beautiful woman. She had long, black, wavy hair and deep, mysterious brown eyes. "Maria Italiana," one of the rebels said, pointing at her.

Another middle-aged woman came running out of the coffeehouse. She spoke to the rebels with great agitation in her voice. She was pointing ahead, down a dirt road. The rebels motioned for the Americans to sit down. "*Sjedni, sjedni.*" ("Sit, sit.") they said as they took off running in the direction the irate woman pointed.

The Italian woman smiled at the newcomers. "Hello, how are you? I am Maria."

"*Buonasera Senorita*" Bob Pastorelli had a chance to try his Italian.

"*Ciao ragazzo, sei italiano?*" Maria responded with a smile pointing at Pastorelli.

"*Sì, lo sono. Ma parlo pochissimo l'italiano,*" Pastorelli had to confess.

"Okay. I speak some English," She responded.

The rest of the Americans introduced themselves. She spoke enough English for the Americans to understand that she was looking for a way out of Yugoslavia and that she was going to join the group walking to the promised land, as she called the secret airport. With her English and Bob's Italian, they managed to ask her if she knew where they were.

"Come here," she said, and she entered the coffeehouse.

A few old wooden tables and straw chairs were standing on the wooden floor. The middle-aged woman behind the counter started talking loudly, waving her hands – nobody knew what she was talking about. Maria shook her head and mumbled something at her, before guiding the Americans to a map nailed on one of the white-washed walls. The woman stopped talking, finally realizing that none of her listeners understood what she was saying.

Maria pointed with her finger to the map. "*Ecco,*" she told the Americans.

She was pointing to the heart of Yugoslavia. It was difficult to know the exact location because the map was written in Yugoslavian. But calling on Shaun O'Brien's sketchy geographical knowledge of the country, he figured she was pointing to the border between Serbia and Bosnia.

"We are entering Serbian territory," O'Brien confirmed. He must have made better grades in geography than some of the rest.

Maria's finger traveled up the map. It stopped at the highest point of Yugoslavia, close to the Austrian border.

"*Penso che tu sia caduto qui*" she said.

Bob Pastorelli explained that she was pointing to the place that their plane was shot down. Maria nodded her head in agreement, "*Sì, sì.*"

"Yes, that is where Lucky Lady went down," Andy Ryker remarked. "That is the territory where we bailed out. We have walked through Slovenia, Croatia, and part of Bosnia," he continued, and he ran his finger in a straight line from the top of Yugoslavia to the place they were now.

"*Dobbiamo andare giù qui.*" ("We have to go down here,") Maria said, pointing farther down.

"Down to Montenegro!" Several men exclaimed, their dismay was evident.

"Well, at least we are halfway there," O'Brien said as he placed my finger next to Andy's and drew it down the map from their current location to Montenegro. From there, the final destination to Lecce was across the Adriatic Sea.

It made sense that they were headed south so as to be directly across from Lecce, Italy. The aircraft would have a short flight, increasing the odds for a safe trip. The aircraft that were used to rescue surviving members of the armed forces were not adequately equipped for combat. In any air-to-air engagement with the enemy, there would be very little chance of survival. The Americans had walked a long way to get here, and they had a long way to go. Loud voices sounded from the outside of the coffeehouse. Everyone stepped outside.

The rebels who were leading the Americans to safety had run down the road and now they were back, bringing with them two men whose hands were tied behind their backs. The four of them argued passionately. The full-figured woman from the coffee house stepped outside and pointed to the two men with their hands tied behind their backs.

"*To su oni! To su oni!*" (That's them! That's them!) She yelled making theatrical gestures, repeatedly.

The rebels yelled at the two men, pointing their fingers in their faces as if they were lecturing them.

The captured men shook their heads, "*Neh, Neh*," they said with terror in their eyes.

The Americans assumed they meant "no" and the only other word understood by the Americans was "Mihailovic."

"*Neh, Neh*," the captured men repeated. But they were not convincing enough.

One of the rebels grabbed the hair of one of the captured men and pulled his head back. With a quick move, before anyone understood what was coming, he pulled a long knife from his waist and sliced the throat of the screaming man. His blood splattered several feet away. The man's body jerked a few times and then fell to the ground with blood pouring out of his neck.

The other man began to shake like a leaf in the wind, pleading for his life. His cries did not move the rebels, and his throat was sliced with the same knife. A couple of feet away, there was a ditch, where the first lifeless body was thrown. The other body was kicked into the ditch next to his friend. It was a gruesome sight. The dead men were Mihailovic's people who had stopped by the coffeehouse for a drink. The lady proprietor had overheard them planning to inform the Germans where Tito's Partisans and the Americans, we're going to pass through German lines that night. Maria explained this as best she could.

The Germans would pay good money in exchange for any information that would lead to the capture or death of Tito's Partisans. They would pay even more for details about Allied airmen. Fighting the Partisans in the mountains was a difficult task. It was easier to ambush them in the valleys at night. The two Mihailovic men had received a different reward than they had expected.

Soon all travelers were ready to go on their way. They jumped over the ditch in which the bodies were lying. Maria walked with the team. She had good energy and tried to keep everyone's spirits high by joking and singing Italian songs. She tried to get them to sing along, but only Pastorelli sang. He apparently knew most of the words and the rest either did not know the songs or they were not in the mood. Farther ahead, the only one who walked by her side and tried to start a conversation, apparently speaking some Italian, was the mostly quiet-man, Clark Bailey.

That night, they had to pass through a relatively large German-occupied city in the valley. Their journey was becoming more dangerous with every step. They were caught between the Germans and Mihailovic's Chetniks. There was not much left of the city. Homes were destroyed, and storefronts closed, either by fallen debris or heavy steel shutters. With the moon's brightness to guide them, they passed through the city, creeping around the German camp. At the far edge of the city, they came to a bridge about twenty feet long. A German soldier guarded each end of the bridge.

The Partisans who were leading signaled them to sit and wait. They were at the foot of a small hill that was covered with trees. Four rebels faded into the darkness around the bridge. Like phantoms, they climbed under the structure, two of them crossing to the other side. There was one German on each side, and it was an easy task for the Partisans to take them out quietly.

One of the Partisans came back and signaled them to move east. They stepped onto the bridge, passing the body of the first German soldier, and began running across quickly and quietly, stepping over the dead body of the second German soldier at the other end. Some of the Partisans were busy installing explosives under the bridge. As soon as the Americans understood their intent, they were off running for the nearest mountain. They were about one-hundred yards away when a tremendous explosion deafened their ears. The air was filled with fireworks.

"*Bježi*! *Bježi*!" ("Run! Run!") the Partisans urged, and they all did, as fast as they could.

12

DEATH IN THE VALLEY

For the next two days, the roving team walked and rested, stopping in little villages for a plate of polenta, then kept going on their way to the promised land. Maria displayed great stamina keeping up with the pace of the team. At least now there was someone who could speak some English and some Yugoslavian and be a bridge of communication between the Americans and the Partisans. In one of the villages, the Americans met a British major. He was tall and thin and wore a patch over his left eye, an eye he'd apparently lost in a battle.

He clarified the situation when he told the Americans, "You are about ten days from your destination."

The major was in British Intelligence and had parachuted into Yugoslavia a few months before. "I am tired of this place. I want to go home," he said. And so, he joined the team. He would not tell anyone his name. "Call me Major," he said.

The day after the team picked up the major, they reached a small valley that had been freshly plowed.

"They are about to plant corn and wheat," the major said.

"Oh great, more polenta," someone responded.

"You see, they have to plant things that grow fast because these people are hungry now." The major explained.

The team entered the valley from a three-hundred foot deep canyon. A stream of unspoiled water ran between the thick foliage of the trees that had sprouted throughout the canyon. The valley was about a mile long and a half mile wide, and it was enclosed by mountains shaped like a horseshoe. Pine trees adorned the slopes. A crystal-clear stream flowed from the top of the mountains down the side of the valley and into the canyon. A few of the Americans stood for a moment to marvel at the beauty around them.

It was late afternoon when they reached the valley. The only sounds that came from the earth were the rolling waters and the chirping of the birds running throughout the canyon. The air stood still and thin; the sun was about to set. Vivid orange lines brushed across the blue sky. The mellow sunlight highlighted a multitude of pine trees, freshly plowed valley, and a green canyon; it was a picture drawn by the hand of a supreme being. The team walked alongside the creek and up into the valley, towards the small village nestled at the foot of the mountain. Its rooftops were snuggled among trees. There was a lot of activity in the village. It was one of the few times that the Americans had seen children, and there was more livestock than in the other villages.

The rebels dispersed the Americans to the various houses whose inhabitants had agreed to give them something to eat. By now, all of them were swimming in their clothes, because they had lost so much weight. It was the usual menu; polenta and an egg. Polenta, which had sustained the Americans for many days, consisted mainly of ground corn, with a little oat straw added for filler. The mixture was boiled in water until it was the consistency of oatmeal.

However, in this village there was something different; the

enticing aroma of baked bread spear throughout the small village. The women in the village had made bread. The bread was made in an inverted cup-shaped pan packed with hot coals around it. The hot bread was a great treat for the Americans. After dinner, the Americas walked back down to the other end of the valley to a small shed. This was a safe place to take a rest.

From afar, gunfire was raging on the horizons beyond the mountains. The British major and Maria told the Americans that there was a brutal battle between the Germans and the Partisans in the valley beyond the horseshoe-shaped mountains. This was the same valley that the team was planning to pass some time during the night. The Germans were trying to come up the mountains, and the Partisans were defending. It was an uneasy feeling for those who wanted to get some sleep. However, no one wanted to be asleep if the Germans came through. The British major noticed their anxiety.

"Don't worry, the Germans have been trying to come up this mountain for four years," he said.

That explained the children and the plethora of livestock in the village; the residents felt secure. The Americans relaxed and slept in the shed until midnight. Then they went back to the village where their guides were waiting, and they began the steep climb up the slope of the mountains at the far end of the valley.

The biting air of the cloudy night urged them to walk fast to keep warm. The group reached the top of the mountain and started downwards on the other side. They were scheduled to enter the German-held valley by three o'clock.

The darkness concealed an eerie mystery as their shadows moved through the high towering trees. The occasional gunfire came from the valley ahead and broke the stillness of the night.

Suddenly rebel guides pushed the Americans behind trees and whispered something. Everyone in the group disappeared behind tree trunks. Two shadows appeared, coming up the mountain. Everyone held their breath. Then the rebels stepped out and began to talk to the newcomers in low voices.

It was then that the Americans realized the two men were Partisans. They began an animated dialogue. Some were pointing toward the valley and others toward the top of the mountain. The team leaders seemed to be urging the two newcomers to go back the way they had come. The battle was still raging down in the valley. It was apparent that the two rivals had attacked one another in bloody chaos.

In battles like this one, the men rolled around in the bloody grass as they savagely slit each other's throats, and they tore each other's bellies. The clash among men lacerated the night. The uproar was from men slaughtering each other over a few inches of land, for ideological differences. And killing, that most ancient need of man, took on a high mystical meaning. Throughout the night there would be flesh against flesh. The guides of the group decided to turn away from these unseen terrors and make their way back down the mountain to the village they had left only hours before. The Americans were told to go back to the shed and rest; they would try again to cross the valley tomorrow night. Using stones for their pillow, the Americans fell asleep. Everyone was awake by seven o'clock and walked toward the village, hoping to find something to eat.

As they walked along the stone houses, machine gun fire suddenly deafened their ears. Bullets ripped the wall between the men. At the same time, several Partisans were running, yelling, and motioning for the Americans to follow them. And run they did - they ran for their lives. By the time they reached the end of the village, all hell had broken loose. There was machine gun fire coming from three different directions. Field mortar shells were landing all around; the explosions were sending lethal shrapnel everywhere. It was an unexpected turn of events. Everyone seemed to be surprised. People were running in pandemonium to the open end of the field.

The night before, the Germans had defeated the Partisans and advanced up the mountain. They had set up their machine guns, mortars, and riflemen along three sides of the valley. Then they waited for daylight.

As the sun rose over the horizon, the Germans set their aim at the Americans and the villagers. They waited until they were all in the village. Then they started firing.

John Mueller reached the open valley beyond the village; he felt that his chances of survival were remote. Ahead of him unfolded a disturbing scene: women, children, and elders were frantically running toward the canyon that lay at the open end of the valley.

Horses and livestock ran along with the people among the mortar explosions. There was also a team of horses pulling a large buckboard wagon loaded with women and children. The men of the village were running behind it trying to shield their women and children from this deadly force, but the explosions and gunfire were relentless all around them.

Mueller had no choice. He threw himself into the rain of gunfire with the rest of the people running to safety. He ran amongst the destruction of iron and fire. After a few steps, he found himself engulfed in smoke, dust, screams and anguish. He ran as fast as he could. A mortar shell exploded to his right;

it landed amid the team of horses pulling the wagon. In his peripheral vision, he saw people and horses lifted several feet into the air and blown to pieces, among them several children. Through the smoke, he saw women now carrying children in their arms in a frantic run to safety. Men were helping the wounded and the elders trying to get away from the fire of death. A chunk of hot metal from an explosion hit Mueller, just above his ankle, taking a piece of meat from his leg. A few yards ahead of him and to his right, spurts of dust from machine gun fire warned him of danger. He hit the ground. On his way down, a small piece of hot metal sheared off a part of one of his knuckles. Most of the machine gun fire was coming from his left. The assault continued relentlessly and without mercy. Lying on the ground, he pointed his feet in the direction that most of the fire was coming from, hoping to make as small a target as possible.

A burst of bullets hit underneath his right arm. Miraculously, he was not hit. Mueller lifted his head trying to spot the rest of the crew. The scene was horrifying. People and animals were falling all around him, blood splattering from their wounds. The freshly plowed soil, darkly rich and ready for seeding, was covered with bodies - some completely still collapsed in death, others mired in pain and fear.

Voices of panic and screams of pain filled the valley.

He spotted Shaun O'Brien and George Poulos who had dropped to the ground several yards behind him. A machine gun bullet hit next to Mueller's left ear, throwing dirt into his face. Another bullet hit his right hand that stretched out flat ahead of him. The same burst carried on and hit O'Brien on the leg.

"I'm hit," yelled O'Brien.

Poulos got on his hands and knees to help O'Brien. A burst

of gunfire hit George and he fell next to O'Brien's body. Beyond the smoke and fire appeared Bill Stoney, he ran to help his fallen crew members.

"Bill, get down, get down," Mueller cried out. But Stoney kept running for his friends.

Another burst of gunfire ripped Stoney's body and he fell on the ground. As he was falling his hands reach into his left pocket and the photograph that was tucked inside of it. Stoney's face hit the ground with both of his hands still clutching the pocket over his heart. Suddenly, Andy Ryker was next to Mueller He was attempting to reach out and help Stoney, but was having trouble to standing up after he was hit in the leg by gunfire.

"Damned you!" Andy Ryker was furious.

Mueller's mind was with his best friend, Bill Stoney. He stood up ready to run to his friend's rescue. Then he'll be back to help Andy. At that moment nothing else mattered; the bursts of machine guns, the mortar bombs - nothing except getting to his good friend.

As Mueller stood up, dazed in shock, and disoriented by the crushing slaughter, he saw a man strolling as if he were going on a Sunday walk in the park. He recognized the uniform - it was the British major.

"Come along, lad," he said.

Mueller looked at him with wonder. How could he be so calm amidst this destruction and death?

"I have to go back, for my friend!" Mueller yelled.

"You can't go back; you will be killed too," the British major replied.

The major's calm demeanor wasn't enough to stop Mueller and he took a few steps towards Stoney.

The major grabbed Mueller's arm. "Listen to me, even if you got out there it would do him no good. The rebels have no medicine. Your friend is severely wounded, if you bring him back, he will die with the Partisans. He has a better chance of surviving with the Germans."

The major was standing amid the carnage as if nothing was happening, carrying on an urgent but subdued conversation. But Mueller was beyond reason. His eyes searched wildly for a clear spot to run and help his friend. The other men were getting out of the way, either crawling or leaping away from the ongoing heavy fire. Only Stoney stayed still. Mueller turned and leaned into the relentless fire from the Germans.

But the major held his arm tight and said, "I told you, the Germans will take care of him. If you run over there, you will be killed too. What is it that you don't understand?"

Mueller looked at the general with skepticism and amazement. Who was this one-eyed man with the black patch over his eye and telling him what to do?

Mueller saw the determination on the major's face. "I am not about to let you go." the major's voice was firm. "Now stay with me, don't run, and don't pay attention to the fire. There is nothing we can do about that. We will continue walking. If the gunners can't see the spurts of dust from where they are, they won't know how close the bullets are landing, and they'll change their aim."

They walked for about a quarter mile under machine gun fire from three directions. It seemed surreal to be walking as though they were on a relaxing walk. Just as the major had said, eventually the sound of gunshots was behind them. They had escaped the slaughter and were too far away for the enemy firing to be effective.

The clear waters of the creek running swiftly next to Mueller were now stained red from the flow of blood. Walking, they reached the end of the valley, they went around a curve, and ran until they dropped from exhaustion. By now, the major and Mueller had put over five miles between them and the Germans, all uphill. The machine gun sounds, the explosions, the screaming people, the blood running in the creek, these images filled Mueller's mind as if it were all a dream, yet he knew otherwise. He cut off a piece of cloth from his heated suit and wrapped it around his wounded leg.

The sun had arrived, scorching the bloodstained land. Its rays spilled through the tree branches trying to lull Mueller to sleep. There would be a moment of rest before the threat of death again fell upon the harsh lives of the people who have grown weary of battles, immune to death. The people who had survived the butchering were now on the run, moving to find a safer land, leaving behind the trees in their courtyards, the songbirds in their cages, the flower pots on their windowsills, the basil and the roses in their gardens. The people had become hard, letting hate simmer inside of them, mute and unrevealed, hate that someday would burst out, insolent and free. Mueller was lying on the very land on which the laughter of the people seemed like an act against nature.

13

NO MAN'S LAND

Voices awoke Mueller. It was and Clark Bailey and Maria. They both looked exhausted but relieved to see familiar faces.

"We are wandering around trying to find the rest of our crew," Bailey said.

The English major was lying on his back, staring up at the sky. "You people should not be wandering around. This is dangerous territory, the crossroads of Partisans and Chetniks," the major said as he stood up. He warned, "It is difficult to tell who is who."

Then the major began an animated conversation with Maria. Sometimes, the Englishman got on Bailey's nerves, with that English accent and the arrogant attitude, but, after all, he did save Mueller's life.

The Major and Maria, merging English and Italian, talked for a few minutes. He was talking, pointing over the mountain, and she was moving her hands more than her lips. After the animated conversation, Maria laughed mockingly, staring at the major and said, "The British, think they know everything."

Then she walked away, shrugged her shoulders, mumbling in Italian and headed downhill.

Clark Bailey and John Mueller looked at each other,

probably thinking the same thing. After the British and Italian argued while trying to decide which way to go, the major pointed to the top of the mountain and said. "We will move south."

Another afternoon of climbing began. Now there were just four of them and they didn't have the rebels to guide them. By the time they reached the top of the mountain, night had fallen. The moon was exceptionally bright that night and seemed so close to the earth. It was lighting their path all the way down to the mountainside. The travelers decided to continue downwards until the mountainside became too steep and dangerous to walk.

They found a spot to rest for a few hours. It was unusually cold that night. The four travelers crawled behind large rocks trying to keep warm. The killings in the valley were haunting everyone's mind. John Mueller thought about his friend Bill Stoney and Andy Ryker. He wasn't sure if they were dead or alive. The image of Bill grasping his picture while falling down played over and over in his head. He thought about Diana, Bill's fiancée, and the child left behind. How would they cope with the loss, how would they survive? Hope and fear collided in his mind. The comforting thought that perhaps the Germans helped his friend gave John some hope, but the idea of the Germans killing him on the spot frighten him – a tormenting roller coaster of emotions. Endless memories with his friend, Bill, were reeling in his mind, from childhood to this adventure. Mueller could not imagine a life without his best friend. He thought about Andy Ryker with whom had become close friends during this ordeal. He would be happy to carry him around once again like he did when both of his feet were injured. The image of Ryker, beyond the thick smoke and fire, with bullets tearing through his legs, when he tried to stand. His legs unstable and trembling could not hold him up. Eventually, Mueller's body, exhausted and aching gave in – his eyes closed, and the gruesome images were no more.

He opened his eyes to a colorless sky. There was a subdued serenity in the universe. The only sound was gentle running water just below the mountain. The major was standing up looking into the far horizon. Maria and Bailey were sitting up talking.

"I can hear water running. I believe we're very close to the river." The English major said.

After about an hour's walk down the mountain, they came to a turn. Shortly after the turn, there was a cliff. Water was pouring down a hundred yards into a wide streaming river. The water was rolling from the top of the high green mountains, twisting like a giant snake, dropping into the deep gorge and disappearing around the next mountain towards the lowlands. Around them, lavish mountains towered majestically. The thick greenery of trees and plants climbed up all the way to the mountain tops while smaller streams twisted around the deep green to merge with the river. It was a spectacular view.

Clark sat on a rock to marvel at the beauty of the earth.

"Beautiful," Maria said with amazement.

Clark looked at the Italian girl with admiration. She seemed determined to tackle this impossible task of survival.

"Why would you want to escape from here?" he asked.

"I have to find my way back to Italy. I have a son who needs me."

The British major helped to translate Maria's broken English. "Why did you left Italy, to begin with?"

"I came here to help the cause, to help the Partisans keep the Germans away from their mountain villages, and to defeat the Chetniks."

She seemed strong-minded, determined to follow her beliefs, involved in a war she could have very well stayed away from it. "But now, I must go back and take care of my son. My mother is getting too old to care for him." It seemed that Maria had taken a likeness to the quiet man.

"We must go through the river," was the major's decision.

"I want to learn Italian. Will you teach me?" Clark asked her as they stood, ready for another long walk.

"Yes, yes, I teach you," Maria said smiling.

Getting down by the water through the steep mountainside was challenging at best. They had to rely on holding onto different plants, trees, and each other for safety. Sometimes they slid down a few yards at a time. At one point, Bailey lost his balance and rolled down the cliff for several yards. Luckily, he was stopped by the trunk of a tree. When the others reached him to help, he said that he was fine, except for a few scratches on his legs. After an adventurous downhill climb, they reached the side of the river. The water was crystal clear and cold. They all took a dip in the river. This was the first bath the two Americans had taken since leaving their base at Lecce. It felt good and despite the icy cold water, they wanted to stay in there for a while. But, the major said. "We must go across the river."

They began their walk across. The other side seemed about fifty yards away.

The river did not seem deep at first; they were up to their waist in water. Once they reached the middle of the river, the current became swift and made it impossible to walk. They had to hold onto one another and were forced to backtrack and return to the shore. They found a big boulder and sat behind it, trying to figure out where to go from here. After a short discussion, they decided to walk alongside the river, and try to find a bridge to help them move across.

As they were getting ready to walk down to the riverside, two men appeared. To the Americans, they seemed like the rebels who had led them throughout the mountains and were glad that they were here to help them find a way across the river. Mueller was ready to come out from his hiding place.

"No, no, no," Maria whispered. "Stay down," she said signaling with her hand to stay put.

After the two men had passed, she motioned that the men would cut their throats if they found them.

"How does she know that," Mueller mumbled.

"I have no clue," Bailey answered with a puzzled expression on his face.

The two rebels walked between a path of several huge rocks by the river.

"Let's wait for a while," the major suggested.

A few minutes went by. The water in the river was rolling towards the lower lands; it was the only sound that disturbed the steel of the afternoon. Suddenly, gunshots were coming from behind one of the rocks. The two rebels started running. From behind one of the rocks, three other men came out running, firing their pistols. The deadly chase along the long bank was intense. The three men were gaining ground on the two rebels who were shooting back as they were running for their lives.

The exchange of gunfire continued, and one of the two hunted men was hit by a bullet and dropped. His friend looked at the fallen man, then looked back to his hunters and dove into the river. The three hunters stood by the riverside waiting for him to come up for air and use him for shooting practice. He came up for air a couple of times and then disappeared into the cold rolling water.

The rebels stood by the dropped man and emptied their pistols into him, while angrily yelling words the Americans could not understand.

Maria stood up and yelled, "Partisans, Partisans!" Her shouts revealed their hiding place.

The Americans were not sure what she was doing, they were trusting that she was right in her assessment that the three men were Partisans. She ran down to the side of the river – the Americans and the major followed her. The three men pointed their pistols in their direction until Maria approached them and spoke with them. Maria was right. They were Partisans.

She spoke to them in Italian; they answered pointing down the river. Their conversation took place next to the man who had bled to death.

"Thank you," Maria said.

The rebels came and hugged Maria's three companions, then they picked up the dead body and tossed it into the river. The two Americans, the British major and the Italian proceeded by the big rocks, while the three Partisans walked the other way, shouting for joy. The four travelers walked by the riverside, between the towering mountains. The universe seemed peaceful; a contrast of feelings from a few moments ago.

"Isn't nature beautiful," the major commented.

"Yes," Bailey answered.

The scenery was not just beautiful; it was breathtaking. The definition of "no man's land" had more than one meaning here. This land, any land, did not belong to the men who were destroying it. Further down the river, there was a bridge. It was one of those swinging bridges.

"You see, you see," Maria pointed to the bridge.

The wind had picked up by now. The bridge swayed under the power of the wind. The travelers had to pass one at a time. Bailey went first to make sure it was safe. Maria followed, then the major and Mueller. The passing was difficult because the bridge was unstable under the wind. They had to hold on to the side ropes tightly before making their next step. The wooden steps in some part of the bridge were decayed and could break under any sudden weight. By the time the four travelers went across the bridge, another day had gone. Maria and the major began another discussion.

The major turned to the Americans and said, "The partisans told Maria that beyond the bridge there is a valley that is sometimes heavily guarded by the Germans at night."

They decided to rest, hiding by the bridge, waiting for midnight to try to cross the valley. Another adventurous day had passed. More people had died. Since he was a child, Mueller was used to feeling alone but now it was different. There was the terrible void of missing his friend, it was an unknown feeling, like a part of himself was dead. His mind went back to the day that he came home from school to find no one there. He did not know where Henry and his mother had gone. So much the better anyway, he enjoyed being alone. A few hours later, a police officer arrived at the house and asked young John to go with him. It was the first time he rode in a police car. He was not sure what was happening, and he wasn't about to ask the friendly police officer who was driving the vehicle. Maybe mother and Henry got into an accident, he thought.

The officer drove to the police station and asked little

John to sit on the bench and wait. He sat quietly in confusion, surrounded by the boisterous, characters arguing with the officers. Little John was surprised to see his father there. His dad picked him up and drove to Aunt Helen's home on the east side of Lansing. During the entire ride, his father did not say a word about Henry and his mother. When they arrived at the house, his father had a heated argument with his sister. "Let me adopt the boy." John heard his aunt Helen say.

"No way, he's my son, I'll take care of him," father answered with anger.

John, now eight years old, sat with patience as people were deciding his future. His father seemed upset. "You are going to stay with your aunt Helen for a while." The young boy had never disobeyed his dad, but this time he felt like he had to stand up.

"Dad, I don't want you to force me stay here, please don't make me," he begged.

"There is no other option my son. When I get back on my feet I will be back to take you."

At that moment John felt an overwhelming feeling of love and empathy for his dad. It was the first time in his life that he felt the need to hug someone - he held his dad, tightly. "There is another choice, dad. Take me to my friend Bill's home. His parents will take care of me."

"I can't do that son; they are strangers to me."

"But dad, every time I am there they treat me like their son. Please, I don't want to stay here."

The Stoneys had a lovely home. They owned a tailor shop, and their business provided a good life for them and they were delighted to take care the young boy. For John, it meant another new school and another group of strange kids. Still, he had no idea where his mother and Henry were at the time. He lived with his friend Bill for a couple of years. Those were some of the best years of his young life.

His father often came to pick him up and tell him that one day they will have their own home. In one of those outings with his dad, John found out that his father was now a fishmonger, selling fish from house to house out of his small Model T truck which he had filled with ice. Later in life, his dad told John that he was embarrassed to take him to the place he lived – a room with three other people, and sometimes he would sleep in his truck. His father eventually told him that Henry and his mother were in jail for illegal activities.

Mr. and Mrs. Stoney had agreed to keep John until his dad got back on his feet. But it seemed like his father had a difficult time getting back on his feet. Times were difficult and every time his father came to see him, he was delighted and hopeful that he would tell him it was time to have their own home. Finally, it happened. John was now ten years old and his dad was able to rent a room with a small kitchen. The size did not matter – it was home and close to his friend and, most important, John did not have to change schools. As a child, John Mueller understood the loneliness of the world around him. His mother was in jail with a man he despised and his father was in a never-ending journey to find himself. The familiar feeling of loneliness overcame his senses once again.

Trails of Tragedy and Triumph

14

THE FEAST

It was past midnight. The rushing river waters and the wild wind that shook the temporary bridge were now reduced to a clear, crisp night that stretched mute and mysterious under a gleaming half-moon. After their short rest stop, the group of four was ready to move south and cross to the German-held valley. As they stood up, they noticed a dim light flashing periodically on and off. The moonlight revealed four silhouettes moving along the opposite river bank towards the bridge. When the group reached the end of the bridge, it became apparent that they intended to cross over.

"We should move out before they cross the bridge," the major suggested.

"No, no, maybe they are friends," Maria said.

The first silhouette moved swiftly, crossing the bridge with ease. After crossing, he stopped at the foot of the bridge, about twenty-five feet away from their hiding place. The next two people crossing the bridge moved at a much slower pace. The last person came across with such confidence as if he had made that crossing many times. When the last man stepped off the bridge, the four sat on the ground and lit cigarettes. After a short while, they stood up, ready to continue their journey.

They were whispering and it was difficult to hear what

they were talking about. Clark tried to ask Maria if they were Partisans. She did not answer, she pressed her index finger to her lips and signaled for Clark to keep quiet. She was trying to listen and seemed a bit perplexed.

Several minutes went by while they were trying to communicate about what would be the smart thing to do. They decided to let them pass. Maria carefully peaked over their hiding rock. The steps of the strangers were growing closer. Their voices were becoming louder. And suddenly Maria stood up and started yelling, "*Cekaj, cekaj. Prijatelji, prijatelji*" (Wait - Friends)

"What is she doing?" The major exclaimed.

Two of the newcomers took a defensive position. Mueller and Bailey, followed Maria and recognized two of the figures. One of them was impossible to miss because of his stature. It was Art Bauer and right behind him was George Poulos. The two others were Partisan rebels.

"*Sono amici,*" Maria shouted with a pleasant voice. The two groups reunited, exchanged handshakes and stories. The Americans asked Art and George if they knew anything about the whereabouts of the rest of the crew. They had no news.

It was time to move on. The group, now expanded to eight people: four Americans, two Partisans an Italian and the Englishmen.

To everyone's surprise, the rebel guides were moving parallel to the river. This was not the way they had decided earlier. The major must have seen the uncertain expression on the American's faces because he began to explain the change in plans. "Parts of the valley are brimming with landmines, which makes it even more perilous to walk inland. This is the longest way but much safer."

The plans were for the group to circle the valley through the woods. After all, they had already been walking for hundreds of miles, so a few extra steps today would make little difference.

The moonlight reflected on the surface of the river water to guide their way.

One of the rebels was ahead of the pack, scouting the best way to proceed. They walked over large rocks, fallen tree leaves, and grass. The methodical sound of their steps in the still of the night kept on as the miles passed behind them. Besides their footsteps, the only sound came from the gently rolling water. No one spoke. As another sunrise approached, they stopped on the top of a hill for a much needed rest. By now, they had become accustomed to long walks and immune to body aches. As they sat on the hilltop, it was as if they sat on the top of the world. Beneath the benevolent sun, the deep canyons, the green valleys, the tall trees, the rolling river twisting around the hills between the vivid green and the wildflowers, all created, a harmonious impression of peaceful elegance. A soft breeze caressed their tired bodies. The spectacular view caused their minds to drift away from the destruction and the massacres taking place in this beautiful land.

"Time to go," someone said. And on they went once again, hiking on the inclines and descending the hills, staying close the riverbanks.

As the sun angled to their right, its bright rays blinded their vision. This was the second day they had gone without a meal. They satisfied their hunger with edible greens found along the trails and they quenched their thirst with water from the river. It was late afternoon when they saw an old building by the riverbank. Its roof had caved in from enemy bombings, and the only standing parts of it were some of the walls. As they approached the building, the travelers saw several airmen camped outside. More airmen were lounging inside the building. These were airmen of the Allies, different nationalities, who had been shot down and were camping here awaiting their chance to be taken out of Yugoslavia. This was an indicator that they were closer to the secret valley, their getaway to the promised land.

The Americans looked around for familiar faces but found none. A seductive aroma of cooked foods filled their nostrils. They had not smelled boiled foods since leaving the air base in Lecce. They followed the aroma down to the riverside. Several rebels were sitting around a fire. Above the fire, was a large pot hanging from a tripod. Inside the pot, was an odd mixture of meats boiling in a white broth.

The major and Maria had followed the Americans there. They also stood with an expression of curiosity and obvious hunger. The rebel stirring the pot turned and looked up at them. "*Tripite*," (Tripe) he smiled, pointing to the pot. The Americans had no idea what that was. All they knew was that they could hardly resist the smell.

"This is tripe soup," the major said. "It is made from the intestines of animals."

No one was listening to him. Whatever it was, their empty stomach was ready for it. One of the rebels stood up, picked up a bowl from the ground, and filled it with the soup.

"*Svida li ti se nesto?*" (Do you like some?) he asked, extending his arm with the bowl.

Mueller thought he would never ask. "Yes, thank you, thank you," he said.

He pulled out a hard piece of bread from a bag and handed it to him along with the bowl. The others were given soup and bread as well. They found a tree and sat in its shadow. Some of the Americans had carved small spoons out of wood along the way – just in case. This was the moment. They pulled their hand-carved spoons from their pocket and slowly began to savor every bite of the feast. Every drop from their bowl was gone.

"I tried to remember the best T-bone steak I ever had. It was no match for this." Mueller commented.

Once they had emptied the precious contents from their bowl, they felt like a wolf whose hunger has been satisfied.

"Well, look who is here."

The familiar voice was music to their ears. It was Bob Pastorelli walking down to the riverside. Everyone smiled and began to ask questions.

"How did you get here?"

"I know people!" he said smiling.

Yes, let there be no mistake about this. It was Pastorelli. After a long conversation, the team spent the night in the roofless house. It was a night of welcoming rest.

In the morning, they hit the trail again. This time, the team veered left of the river. Their best guess was that they were moving southeast. They now had three new rebels as their leaders and of course, Bob Pastorelli joined the traveling group. From the top of the hill, they could see the river, the greenery, the hills, befitting a postcard – they were leaving it all behind. Ahead of them spread a large forest, sheltered by hills and tall mountains.

They headed downhill. Their guides asked the rest to walk directly behind them, to follow their footsteps. It was obvious that this area was full of landmines. They were now into the dense woods. The rebel leading the pack raised his hand, signaling for everyone to stop. Another rebel pointed to the ground with an urgency. They all obeyed, and hit the ground, shielding themselves behind trees. The Partisan rebels scattered around and hid behind the thick tree trunks, positioning themselves in strategic spots.

The minute passed in anticipation. Footsteps were heard, approaching from the right. One man appeared. He walked slowly, scouting the ground. Two more men followed a few steps behind. The Partisan leader, the one in the front of the pack, signaled to his comrades to wait for his orders. The rest of the group stayed still. Two more men appeared, following the three others. The Americans could not see any difference between the Partisans and the newcomers. The team of five walked slowly among the trees. The man in the front was about twenty yards away.

The Partisans aimed their M1s and fired. The gunshots echoed through the woods, along with the screams of the ambushed Chetniks desperately calling for their comrades to take cover.

Two Chetniks rebels dropped to the ground. They were the first and the last men of the formation; one of them was crawling with great difficulty, the other was laying still – one wounded, the other dead. The bullets coming from behind the trees crossed between the two teams of combatants.

The Americans, Maria and the major, dug their faces into the ground, as bullets whistled over them. The firing continued intensively for a few moments. The Chetniks were dug into their positions. One of the Partisans crawled to his left, trying to find a position to fire at the enemy. Another one pulled out a hand grenade and let it fly. After the explosion, two of the Chetniks started to retreat. One of them suddenly stopped as if his foot was glued to the ground. The other one was hidden behind a large rock. One of the Partisans told the rest to hold their fire. He had a smile on his face.

"I'll wager that man has stepped on a mine," the major whispered. "He dares not move, or the mine will explode."

They watched the rebel destined to die. He had turned to look back for help - terror on his face.

The Partisans team leader raised his rifle and aimed. Was this to be a merciful killing? Maybe he was aiming at the man's heart, so he would die before exploding. But that was not to be. The Partisan aimed at the right foot, the one stepping on the landmine. The impact of the bullet moved the man's foot. Fire and dirt erupted from the ground. There was a human cry as pieces of stones, dirt, and body parts exploded into the air. Then, there was an eerie silence.

"*Ubojice*!" (Killers) A voice cried from behind the rock. The Chetnik who was hiding behind it stood up and began to shoot his rifle. He was frantic, shooting and yelling. He ran out of ammunition and pulled out his revolver, and shot until it too was empty.

The Partisans waited until the man had no more ammunition and began to shoot at him. The frantic rebel was hit several times, yet he refused to drop.

"*Ubojice*! *Ubojice*!" he kept screaming, as more bullets ripped through his body.

He finally dropped to the ground, into the darkness of death. Everyone waited until it was quiet. The hand grenade supposedly killed the fifth man. The Partisans were careful to make sure that their enemy was eliminated.

One Partisan stood beside one of the Chetniks laying on the ground and emptied his rifle at him. Apparently, this one was still alive. Then he wanted everyone to get moving. A strange sensation overcame everyone not used to this kind of butchering, as they were passing the dead Chetniks. The image of the man blown to pieces from the land-mine stayed intact in their minds. Such manifested hate between humans saddened their hearts. All the training and theories about wars count for nothing when you see people's lives ending in such gruesome ways.

By sundown, they reached a small village on the slopes of a hill. The homes on the hill were buried under the tall trees. The village seemed deserted. Some of the houses were burned and others were looted and destroyed.

"Chetniks, chetniks" said one of our leaders, pointing to the burned homes.

The rebels checked the few homes for people, alive, wounded or dead. There was no one. The Partisans conversed for a few minutes, then motioned everyone to follow them. They walked for about half an hour under the tall trees. The rebels were searching for something.

"What are they looking for?" Mueller asked the major, who seemed to know everything.

"I expect they are looking for dead bodies," he said.

They found nothing in that direction. They turned back, passed through the deserted village, and walked the opposite way. The rebels led, and the rest followed. They were not far from the village when an awful stench hit their nostrils. The rebels at the head of the team covered their faces with their neckerchiefs. They all walked deeper into the stench. The rebels stopped at the edge of a deep hole, and one of the rebels looked at the foreigners.

"*Dodi ovamo!*" (Come here) he motioned for everyone to come closer.

As they approached, the stench became unbearable.

Everyone covered their mouths and noses with their shirts. As they reached the edge of the hole, what they saw inside was difficult to describe. Bodies of men, women, and children were piled up one on top of another. Their bodies were deteriorated; some had been partly eaten by ravens.

They all turned their heads. Impossible to look any longer. Stomachs were turning, and hearts were saddened beyond expression. On the top of the trees, vultures were flying. They were blackbirds of death. Their songs were a monotonic sounds of hunger for human flesh.

Maria held a tree and emptied the little food that she had in her stomach. "*Perché, perché, le persone fanno questo?*" (Why, why, people do this?) she cried.

The Americans walked away from the stench. Their hearts were bleeding with sorrow. The vision of the bodies inside the hole roared in their minds, nesting in their consciences. Impossible to be forgotten. Cruelty of this kind was merely incomprehensible – it was the horrid consequences of war.

"*Vidis. Moras reci,*" (You see. You must tell,) one of the rebels kept saying.

The major and Maria tried to explain to the Americans that they had to tell everyone about these atrocities. Even though the Americans owe their lives to the Partisans, even though what they just saw filled them with anger, this was a war between two irregular armies. They were two teams of people who saw an opportunity to grasp a bit of power, so they could promote the political agenda of their superiors. People whose children, not long ago, had played together, were now killing the sons and daughters of their countrymen. No, this was a war that did not concern them. They had to stay focused and fight their war. For this, the Americans had to get back to their base in Lecce, Italy somehow. Their leaders decided that they had to camp for the night in the deserted village. The night was restless and creepy, knowing that not that far from them there was a hole with dead bodies in it.

15

DEEP ROOTS

Several years after the war ended, Bob Pastorelli took a trip through the streets of his old neighborhood. He found a few structural changes but the cultural customs, the family values and the love for the Italian tricolor flag, the white, red and green, a symbol of the deep roots of their ancestors, remained frozen in time. There were great memories from his childhood. His old school was just four blocks from the house he grew up in, on West Flournoy Street. He remembered the Lucca Bakery where he often went to buy hot-out-of-the-oven bread and custard filled long johns with chocolate icing on Sundays. Then there was the butcher shop, where his mother sent him to get one-pound of ground beef. His mother gave him instructions; "Tell Rocky to ground the beef right in front of you." Funny thing when he goes to buy ground beef now he asks the butcher to grind it fresh. There was the drug store on the corner of Harrison and Western and the candy store, a heaven-on-earth for the children, on the corner of Western and Alley.

Bob often spoke to his friends while trekking the mountains, about those days with a bit of an Italian accent to his voice and with a nostalgic glance. It was clearly understood that the memories were priceless, and the strong sense of cultural identity was unmistakable. He spoke about the butcher as if his mother's dominating character was vivid in his mind, and about the bakery with the desire to taste those fresh-made long johns once again.

As he kept walking in the neighborhood, the old house was still there, but Rocky the butcher, a big bald man in his late forties was long gone. The old bakery, the drug store and candy store have given their space to other businesses, but the old school was still standing protecting innocent secrets and life-long memories. There were many other memories impossible to erase from Bob's mind, like the irresistible smells of freshly baked bread dispersing its aroma to the small streets and the drugstore counter with the soda fountain and the greatest milkshakes a child could dream. There was a fainted smile when he spoke about his mother's commands which he unquestionably obeyed because he knew full well that you could disregard anything else in life, but the only one you never disobey is your Italian mother – what she said was the law of the land.

He was reminiscing about the shop of Marco, the florist, displaying colors and sprinkling aromas on Western Avenue. Across the street, on the corner of Harrison and Western, the barber was on the first floor of the Goodwill building, it was where people went to hear the news. No newspaper needed in the old neighborhood, just a couple of hours in the barber shop and you were up-to-date with local and international news. It was the same place kids got their haircuts. There were no long-layered, slicked, Mohawk, faux-hawk or spike haircuts – just one style, short crew-cut, until high school when the hair grew a bit longer. A little further on Harrison street there was Morizzo funeral home. It was widely known that Mr. Morizzo was the biggest donor to the church.

Further down, still standing, was the Elmo theater, with the "Now Showing" blue and white marquee movie sign, now displaying names like Pat O'Brien, The Marx Brothers, Marlon Brandon, Humfrey Bogart, Elizabeth Taylor, Grace Kelly, Sophia Loren and other mega movie stars. Back when he was a kid, they would make money for candy and a movie by going through the alleys and picking up pop bottles to take to Bill's grocery store and then selling them them for two cents each. With one dime you could buy a lot of candy.

Bob remembered Doctor Burgen well. It was where he would rush in when he was injured. One time he was running holding a pencil, fell on it and the pencil penetrated his skin next to his eyeball. Doctor Champagne, their family doctor's office, was outside of the neighborhood, so Bob walked to Dr. Burger's office. The doctor took a look and told young Bob that, "This is going to hurt. Here bite on this leather wallet. I have to stitch you up." The doctor took care of it. But that was not the difficult task; now Bob had to face mother's wrath.

On the corner of Lexington and Western, there was still the Minelli brothers grocery store with a doorway leading to the little bar in the back. There was Golden's tavern and the Spaghetti Company on Lexington and Claremont. He remembered accordions playing music and voices serenading a secret lover in the moonlight under a window. The old neighborhood was always busy. Peddlers were plenty and colorful. The produce truck was making many stops through the neighborhood displaying beef, vegetables and fruits. It was like an open-air market as housewives bargain for fresh produce and better prices. Kids gathered around the ice-truck to watch the wide-shouldered ice-man lift a big, brown, leather flap that covered the open back of his truck. The cool air, surged out from inside into the heat of the day and put a smile on their faces. Ice blocks were stacked on wooden pallets, the big man used his long, heavy hook to move the blocks of ice and then he would wrap a large piece of leather around the block of ice and throw it over his shoulder to carry it into the customer's wooden refrigerator.

On the weekends some of the older people will listen to soccer matches broadcasted on their radio. Passionate fans divided between the teams of Milan and Juventus. Temporary animosity would fill the air, the fans whose team lost seemed to always blame the referee. Others would play cards or bocci and some would argue politics. The old-timer junk-man had no schedule. He showed up periodically with his wooden wagon pulled by the gray-speckled old horse. Everyone knew he was just down the street when they heard the sound of his voice, "*Ragalia, Ragalia.*" People rushed, gathering old copper or any other worthy metal to sell. If you are looking for the word "*Ragalia*" in the dictionary, it does not exist. The junk-man was actually chanting, "Rags, old iron!"

He was remembering the familiar sound of the red sharpening cart's wooden wheels grinding slowly against the street, its bell ringing and the voice of the thin, older man pushing it, asking for knives and scissors to be sharpened. The watermelon truck's overloaded back had to be empty by the end of the day, so the Spanish-accent driver would pass out deals "Two for a quarter." His voice penetrated through the narrow streets in the quiet afternoons. The Jewish man with his step-van would display clothes on little hooks and people bargained for better prices. Some wanted credit until their payday from work. The Jewish man would check their credit in his I-owe-you-book, a worn-out small ledger filled with "20 cents and 30 cents" charges.

There was excitement in the air at the sound of the ringing bells. The ice cream truck was on its way. Mothers scrambled to find change, children ran out from their homes joyfully towards the young good-looking Italian man. The twinkly-faced young girls looked at him, whispering between them, some young wives would give a passing glance or two towards the white truck, while others would start a conversation. "How are you Frankie? Still working the truck.?" He would smile and say, "It is temporary. Someday I will be a famous singer."

"How is the ice cream, Frankie?"

"It is not like Gelato, but pretty close."

Bob imagined the neighborhood a bit different. Perception is a beast that lives in the mind, torn between romanticism and realism. But, as he walked the streets, there were jasmine, white lilies and violets on the balconies. Basil and tomatoes in most backyards. Smells of fried calamari and the sweet aroma of tomato sauce, was still omnipresent. And now, there were the romantic voices of Domenico Modugno and Mario Lanza, filling the minds of the elders with nostalgia of the old country. Those familiar silky voices, soared out of vinyl record players, to fill the air of the narrow streets with classic Italian songs like *Arrivederci Roma, Volare, and Al di la*. The old park was now overcrowded with dreamers, to someday pitch like Fergie Jenkins or hit home runs like Williams and Santos, and play like Ernie Banks. Surviving life in the old neighborhood was challenging but the small celebrations made life bearable. There were Italian and American flags waved in the air during holidays and the storefront names on the signs were mostly Italian. There was even a man with his pony roaming the neighborhood giving rides to children. On the weekends the parks were filled with children playing and adults watching.

There was an ongoing effort to keep the ethnic and family traditions while away from their motherland. And so, now, nothing has changed about the human struggle to overcome the ongoing challenges of surviving in the periphery of Little Italy in Chicago, a little country in the middle of the vast megalopolis surrounded by endless suburbs that seemed a world away, both in distance and culture.

"My mother used the leftover bread, wet it with water, sprinkled it with salt, pepper, oregano, olive oil and vinegar and there it was - vinegar bread." Bob would say to his traveling companions while trekking the mountains, hungry and exhausted. Back when he was growing up in the old neighborhood, Bob's family lived in two-flat home. The residents on the bottom floor were his cousins. Bob's parents were in one bedroom, his older brother and himself shared a bedroom and his young brother with his sister in the other bedroom. In the middle of the living room there was an oil-stove for central heating and beyond the kitchen and dining table, on the back porch was the wooden ice box. His mother and father belonged to a poker club. Kids were not allowed to go out at night during the week but on the weekends, they left home at ten-o'clock in the morning and came back just before dinner. They were out on the streets playing baseball and other games. During the hot months they turned on the fire hydrants to cool off, their bodies splashing in the water flooding the streets. The hydrants were locked-up by the city, but the kids made a special tool to unlock them. In the old neighborhood everybody knew everyone.

Bob's grandparents, his aunts, his cousins, the entire family was within five blocks from each-other. On Sundays everyone will go to grandmother's house. She usually made mostaccioli, pork neck sauce, beef meatballs, and *pan di spagna* – an Italian sponge cake. His grandparents spoke English very well. Bob's parents were first generation but if they did not want their children to hear something, rather than spelling the word, they spoke Italian.

"I remember being able to walk everywhere. I remember when my wife, Mary, came to Chicago for the first time, she was shocked on how close the homes were, so close we could climb up the buildings, with the palms of our hands on each building's wall. Coming from Arizona, she had never seen back alleys and couldn't comprehend how people lived so close to one-another." Bob told the story often to his traveling companions during their incredible adventure.

He also told the story on how he met his wife when he was in basic training in Luke Field in Glendale, Arizona.

After the war, Bob tried to live in Arizona for a while but his memories, his soul was in little Italy. He convinced his wife to move back. Crowning on Taylor street he was infused with Italian pride, hearing stories of the old country, seeing hard working people, honest, ethical, putting family first, he couldn't help but admire them and be proud.

"A few homes away from my home lived Mrs. Spada. Grandmother always called her a witch and said to stay away because she could give you the evil eye. - Don't go near her, she is a *strega* and could give you the *Malocchio, capisci*?" My Nonna would say.

That is how Bob grew up. He would walk down the street when it rained with paper on the bottom of his shoes to keep the water out. "I had a pair of old galoshes and when I lost one I was out of luck. It was a great way to grow up. Life was simple not a lot of cars on the street. I had my brothers hand me downs, a bike, school shirt and ties. I know what is like to have something and I know what is like to have nothing."

This attitude helped him overcome the loneliness and the hunger on the mountaintops – this and the love of his country, a country that gave his forefathers a chance for a better life. A concept very familiar to George Poulos, since he grew up in a similar culture but lived in New York, hundreds of miles away.

16

DANCE WITH ME

The rays of the morning sun told the team that it was time to move out of the roofless house and onto the road of return. The Americans had lost count of the many hills and mountains they had climbed to descend into the next valley. How long were they looking for a village to ease up their hunger, a forest to hide, a river or a waterfall to quench their thirst? On the other hand, there were plenty of beautiful spring flowers for an ephemeral mending of their spirit, a spirit injured by the ugliness of human tragedy and the horror of savage deaths. The vision that was permanently engraved in their minds was survival; to reach the land of deliverance. They felt that with each one of their steps they were a step closer to freedom. Hope was what made their daily marathon-walk bearable.

The endless miles that the Americans had left behind infused them with strength and confidence that they were capable of doing that much more. The new sun did not bring uncertainty but hope. Here and now was the place and time that they realized that the human spirit could triumph over extraordinary circumstances. It was early morning as the team began their exploration into the woods. The foliage of the trees was dense and hung low in their path, the branches of the bushes sprang long and thick – this turned their walk through the woods into an unusually slow pace. Everyone was tired this morning - this was another day that they went without food. Occasionally there were wild rabbits and deer running through the woods. The rebels lifted their guns, pretending to shoot, but they never did. They knew that gunshots would give away their position to the enemy. Walking in the woods without being detected was a test of strength, a mental torment along with physical torture. It became unbearable at times, but still, none of them wavered in their belief that they would come out of this alive.

As the dusk of the day was approaching, they began to search for a place to rest. The dense woods were starting to thin out. The rebel leaders pointed to a clearing and indicated that this was to be their home for the night. The mountains around them laid their shadows as the sun tilted into the western horizon. Soon, darkness blanketed the earth and most of the men fell asleep.

A chorus of singing voices ascended from afar. The melodies penetrated Clark Bailey's ears – was he dreaming? He opened his eyes. A bright moon was now hanging from a sky studded with countless stars. Strangely, the chorus of voices continued. The sleeping bodies around him began to move and were awaken as well.

"What's going on?" the men would ask with sleepy voices.

They all stood up, uncertain what to do next. Behind them was the dense woods, gunshots, and landmines. There was a brimful chorus of singing voices in the hills ahead of them. The dilemma was which way to go. Clark Bailey turned to get advice from their leaders. They were nowhere to be found. Maybe the major or Maria would know.

To his surprise, they were gone as well.

"Where is everybody?" There was no answer.

"Should we go and find out what is happening out there?" Bailey asked.

Bob answered, "I don't know. I would hate to be separated from our leaders."

"Maybe they went to scout out the area where the voices are coming from," George suggested.

They decided to wait. The four Americans waited for about half an hour. The singing and joyful voices from the hills continued – it sounded like a great celebration.

Finally, the Americans decided to move toward the hills. Soon, they were out of the woods. An array of hills encircled them. On the foot of one of the hills, to their left, silhouettes were dancing under the moonlight.

"I wonder what this is all about?" Bailey asked.

"Maybe the war is over," Mueller replied.

A ray of hope entered their hearts. Was it possible? They had been isolated from the civilized world for about a month now. It was a time without news about the progress of the war.

"Should we go and ask?" Art Bauer suggested.

"We don't even know who those people are. For all we know they might be Chetniks," George Poulos cautioned them.

They stood for a few moments, undecided what to do next. The voices and the rhythmical clapping created a festive atmosphere. It had been awhile since anyone of them had heard happy sounds and seen joyful people. Everyone was curious to find out about the dancing shadows on the hill. The fact that the Americans had lost their leaders made their decision easier - go to the hill.

"We must be careful," Bailey warned. The five men approached the hill. Their hope was that the Englishman, Maria, and their leaders, would be somewhere among the people by the hill. They reached the foot of the hill. On its slope was a plethora of tall trees. The clapping, the shouts of celebration and the singing voices were now deafening.

"What do you think, guys? Should we move up?"

"Why not? We need a little entertainment."

Slowly they approached the back of the short hill and climbed its slopes. They could feel the vibration of the singing voices and the foot thumping of dancing people. As they reached the top of the hill, they were surrounded by dozens of jubilant people. No one seemed to pay any attention to their presence. At the bottom of the hill, there was a tiny valley. Around the valley towered other hills forming a natural amphitheater. Directly below the Americans, there were four musicians; two of them on each side, playing their clarinets. The other two were in the middle, one playing the tanpura and the other playing the gusle. In front of the band of musicians there was a woman holding a tambourine and singing. There was dancing in the amphitheater's floor and more people were sitting on the grassy slopes – this was a great festive scene; people celebrating with songs and dancing. The Americans were mesmerized by the energy of the people. "Guys, these are Partisans. I recognize some of our guides." Mueller said. That is all they needed to hear. They stood up and headed down the hill. They were greeted with cheers and pats on the back.

The Americans walked through the animated crowd, found a spot by the hillside and sat down. Clark Bailey figured that since he was unable to comprehend the meaning of this celebration, he might as well enjoy the entertainment. George Poulos would have none of that – this was his element. He walked onto the stage and joined the circular dancing chain. The dance was similar to the ones performed by the villagers in the panegyrics of Greece. Whistling and shouts of "Opa" filled the air – it seems like everyone knew what "Opa" meant.

Suddenly Clark Bailey spotted Maria among the dancing people. She was dancing with gusto and seemed to be full of joy. Their eyes met – she smiled. "Come on Clark." She waved her hand calling him to join.

"No, no, that's okay," he replied. Dancing was the furthest thing from his mind. Maria stepped towards Bailey, "Come on Clark. Dance with me!"

Clark could not resist. "I don't know how to do this dance."

"It's nothing, just follow my steps," Maria said as she joined in the circular dance. "What is the occasion?" Bailey asked.

"Victory, victory! Partisans have Chetniks on the run, no more Chetniks!"

There was a triumphant expression in her voice as if this was her victory. As for Bailey, he was glad for the Partisans and their help, but the big war was still on, as far as he knew. Their safety, across the Adriatic Sea, was still far away. The situation in Yugoslavia was now becoming clearer. Tito's forces were in control. Military support from the allies and the success of the Partisans brought Tito closer to political power. By now the Serbian guerrilla forces under General Draza Mihailovic were defeated in Herzegovina and Montenegro, and Mihailovic was forced to retreat to the Serbian mountains with the remnants of his command. Now the main concern were the Germans.

Suddenly there was silence. Bailey's thoughts were

interrupted. The musicians were about to take a break. George Poulos walked to the musicians and asked if he could use one of the clarinets. The group of dancers remained on the floor – curious to find out what was coming next. George raised the clarinet and began to weave a mournful melody on the still air. The emotions of the people increased with the volume of the song. George raised his clarinet towards the heavens as if he was aiming for the ears of God. The beautiful sound cut across the eerie silence of the mesmerized people. Suddenly, there was a sorrowful, deep humming following the music – more and more voices joined the chorus and like the prayers of a cantor, they too aimed towards the heavens. And then, a rhythmic clapping joined the chorus of hundreds of mouths. The atmosphere was electrifying. The other musicians joined George and began to increase the tempo of the music. On the floor of the natural stage, people began to dance. Some in groups, others by themselves.

The morning was near. The tempo of the celebration had not lost its energy. Maria and Clark were inseparable during this celebration dancing, laughing and talking. Eventually the celebration faded away and everyone had to go their way. One thing was certain, no one was going to look at George the same way. For the Americans, it was time to continue their quest to find their safe ground and hopefully from there go on to Italy.

The morning after the celebration, the Americans joined a group of airmen, wanderers like them. The one-eyed British major was there but Maria wasn't. "Where is Maria?" George asked Clark Bailey.

"I am not sure," Clark replied, "maybe she'll join us later." His voice was notably sad.

"Keep moving south. Your leader knows the way," The

British major said.

"And you, Major?" Mueller asked.

"I'll stay for a while," he said. He did not smile, but he seemed less grim than usual.

"Thank you for saving my life," Mueller said, as he saluted the major and then shook his hand. After that, the expanded team headed south.

Trails of Tragedy and Triumph

17

BIRD OF PASSAGE

The new leaders guided the team of airmen southbound. The echo of the songs and the hand clapping remained nested in their ears for a while. Clark Bailey looked at the men walking alongside him; He saw a hero behind each unshaven face. Those weren't men who walked with tired steps, ripped clothes and shoes full of holes as their only possessions; they were giants whose spirit of survival soared to incredible courage. Enormous pride rose in his heart to be in the company of such men.

Along the way, more coalition airmen joined the group. Soldiers who had survived miserable conditions, anxious to reach the land of deliverance. It was now a gathering of over forty people. Some of the people in the group were critically wounded. There was an Italian carrying another man on his back, piggyback. The man being carried was barely breathing. The man who carried him was determined to bring him home alive.

"*Siamo quasi là*,"(We are almost there) he kept repeating as he struggled to keep his balance with every step.

George, Bob, Clark, Art and John, the five crew members of Lucky Lady, were walking along with this group of wanderers. The whereabouts of the other crew members were unknown. Hopefully, they were with similar teams headed in towards the same direction.

It had been two days since the night of the panegyric atmosphere as the large group of survivors continued to hike over mountains and pass through small valleys. The fact that they had not seen any Germans in these valleys was encouraging and peculiar.

"The Germans are moving all of their forces to bigger cities," one of the airmen commented.

After a steep and challenging climb, they reached the top of another hill. Looking down the southern slope, they could see a large town, severely damaged by bombing and battles. The going was easier as they descended into the valley.

Walking through the ruins of the streets, they saw only a few buildings with their roofs attached. The front steel shutters of the shops were either blown off or bowed.

The smell of death and the picture of absolute devastation was disturbing. Their leaders guided them through narrow streets riddled with large holes and littered with piles of rubble. The stronger survivors have taken turns to occasionally help carry the injured men. The Italian airman, dragging his feet, was again carrying his friend on his back. Though he staggered under the heavy load, he displayed tremendous strength and courage.

"*Siamo qui! Siamo qui!*" (We're here! We're here!) he kept saying to his comrade.

While the team moved through the destroyed town, a strange sensation came over Clark Bailey. At that moment he felt that he belonged to neither world. Behind him was the devastation of human tragedy.

Ahead of him, was the anticipation of human triumph.

As the dusk of the ending day blanketed the ruined city,

a colorful giddiness enveloped Clark's mind, as he thought of Maria. A loud voice of hope kept urging him to move on, to leave behind the ruined world composed of hate and misery. Dark unyielding mysteries of the past were pounding in his mind, a mind that remained thirsty to discover the celebrations of life, away from this horrifying human tragedy. And there was Maria's alluring smile stimulating his heart.

With every step, with every inch of ground he covered, the human misery seemed to fade into the background as he approached the land of deliverance.

At the far edge of the deserted town, an American colonel appeared from one of the buildings that still had a roof. He warmly welcomed the team of survivors.

The men were taken into a building and given something to eat. The colonel informed everyone that this town was the end of their journey and that from a secret airfield they were going to be airlifted back to their base.

The Americans could hardly grasp the meaning of his words. Finally, they were under allied control, after more than a month of danger and hardship, and they were overjoyed. Everyone stared at the officer, unsure of what to do next.

"Find a place to rest," the colonel said.

They were housed in a two-story building that seemed to be an old hotel because it was divided into several small rooms. Of course, there was no furniture anywhere in the building. Once inside the men from Lucky Lady were requesting information on the whereabouts of the rest of their team. Nobody knew. Finally, fatigue overcame all other impulses and most of them crushed into a peaceful sleep. Clark Bailey had found a spot in the upstairs flat and laid on the floor to rest. Bailey was well respected by his companions. He was known as a quiet man, someone composed and clear-sighted, but no one really knew much about his early life. When he was asked about his family, he simply said, "My father is a gambler and my mother is a saint."

Clark Bailey loved nature and engines, and he was well versed in history and philosophy and well-mannered. Clark's life has been significantly touched by his father's gambling. His father, Charles, grew-up as an orphan and spent his childhood in-and-out of various foster homes in Chicago. At the age of sixteen, he was able to earn a living by playing pool for money. At first, he used the common hustling method; a misleading act of disguising his skill with the intent of luring another player into gambling for higher stakes. However, he soon realized that the hustler's stereotype wasn't suitable for his personality. During the nineteen-twenties there was a plethora of pool halls in Chicago. There were over a dozen of them in the Chicago loop alone. This was where most of the pool hustlers hung out. Pool hustlers use to disguise themselves as regular working people, or drunk, or just learning to play. They would go from room to room to find a "mark" - a person easy to be hustled. The pool hustlers had a "bird dog" in every action room - someone that would tip them off when a "mark" walked in. Usually the person to hustle was a wise guy flashing his money.

Young Charles thought that pool hustlers give a bad name to the beautiful game - he always thought himself as a professional gambler. Charles decided to travel from city to city, going west by train, shooting pool to earn money, but now he had changed his ways. He began to provoke the ego of the regulars who thought themselves best in the room. He used psychology as an alternative to hustling. He would walk into a room and say,

"My name is Charles Bailey, I am a professional gambler and I am here to play with the best but, I am warning you that I will take your money!"

Beaumont's farming, lumber and later on its shipping industries created a blossoming economy in the city. The discovery of oil on the nearby Spindletop increased the Beaumont's population by the thousands. The mill economy was also on the rise and well-paid jobs attracted many new residents to the city, many of them immigrants. Clark Bailey's father choose to stay in Beaumont because most of the residents had extra money for entertainment and gambling. Bailey's father met his future wife at a barbecue party, married her and stayed. He was upfront with her about who he was and what he did for a living, but she didn't care, she was madly in love with him. So, Margaret and Charles became Clark's parents and gave him a younger brother as well. Clark Bailey grew up in Beaumont, a city of Southeast Texas, on the Neches River and a couple of hours drive east of Houston. For his father, Charles Bailey, gambling was the only order in his life, the only thing he knew.

Clark's father claimed no relatives, no roots, no other vices. He disdained womanizers, drugs and boozers. He was well dressed, always wearing a tie and he was polite, cool and good-looking, and he was unbeatable while stroking a pool cue. During the booming economy of the roaring twenties Charles would take his young son, Clark with him. The two of them would travel to different cities, scout the pool halls and go to work making big scores. They traveled by train to Dallas, Houston, New Orleans and Tulsa Oklahoma. They stayed a couple of days in each town playing long games for big money with the best pool player. They would go back home and spend a few days with the family.

Clark's dad made sure that his mother had money to maintain their household and then on to Philadelphia and Baltimore, and sometimes as far as New England, Buffalo and Montreal.

When the great depression came along, most people had no money to gamble. It was then that Clark's father turned to cards, dice and sports betting but that was not his element and he had the discipline to quit and go back to do what he did best – shooting pool for money.

Clark's mother was a devoted Christian woman, a saint accepting her husband's lifestyle and loving him dearly. His father was faithful and kind to his wife until the end. Clark's mother's heart was an ocean of love. She found solace in God, while his father's sole satisfaction was the pool table. Clark and his young brother Paul grew up in a peaceful house. The stories about their father's pool-hustling trips throughout the United States and Canada, shooting pool with the local masterful billiard players, were endless and fascinating. Clark Bailey had learned many lessons from his parents. His father taught him about risk and what it means to live on the edge. His mother taught him patience and devotion to those you love. He had learned that freedom entails risks and security requires compromising some individual freedoms; you can never have both.

18

ANTICIPATION

Groups of survivors were lazily sitting around the building talking, sharing stories, anticipating the moment of freedom. It felt odd that they did not have to get up and begin walking again. George Poulos was sitting outside, talking with Mueller and Bauer, all around them were the many other coalition airmen waiting anxiously for destiny to take its course. They were anxious to hear their name announced to board the airplane back to Italy.

"Amigos" that familiar booming, happy, voice was unmistakably Cardenas. Mueller and Bauer turned around to see Manny Cardenas, his arms wide open and smiling, "I am here Amigos." he exclaimed.

There were joyful shouts and a lot of questions. Cardenas explained that after the massacre in the valley, trying to escape the fire, he was separated from everyone. He roamed around the woods, at night and found a safe place to rest. The following day he met a group of six people, two Partisans and four airmen, on their way to the secret airport. One of the Partisans was fluent in Spanish and kept him informed of what was happening. "In every village along our way they told us you were a couple of days ahead."

The second day went on uneventfully. They all waited impatiently in anticipation of being called for liftoff standby. George felt fortunate that he was one of the few to reach this secret liftoff location. This place was the gateway to freedom, a place where all rescued airmen were taken to be airlifted back to various locations in Italy. Thousands of airmen did not make it to this airfield. Their lives ended in the steep mountains and the dangerous valleys. George thought of the many other people whose lives had been affected by this war. In this destroyed city, waiting to be taken back to their base, there were no natives. Certainty there was a life here before the war. The original inhabitants of the city were either dead or had been taken away to German forced labor camps.

An announcement by a young airman interrupted George's thoughts. The young airman was reading the list of people on today's liftoff roster. George heard his and Mueller's name called. Today it was his turn to be excited. It was eleven o'clock that night when, along with thirty-one others, George and John Mueller walked the two miles down to the valley airfield.

It was a night covered with fog, and the sky was loaded with dense clouds.

Their trek over the rough terrain was tiring. They reached the airfield and were ordered to wait on the east side of the field. The hidden airfield was a grassy valley surrounded by high mountains. George wondered how a C46 could land in that valley, coming over the steep mountain tops. The pilot would have to have extraordinary skills to be able to land an aircraft in that field successfully. The dark clouds hung so low that they covered the mountaintops. The fog was thick and did not allow him to see beyond the middle of the airfield. There was no possible way that an aircraft would be able to land under these conditions. But he did not give up hope. All the chosen survivors who were about to be lifted up and taken back, stood intently, listening for the sound of an airplane.

The familiar drone of the C46 engines sounded above the dark clouds and soon it was directly overhead. The commander of the team shot up a red flare. The red flare indicated to the pilot that visibility was terrible, and the landing had to be canceled. The fleeting disappointment was replaced with renewed hope that the next midnight a landing would be successful. They hiked back to wait for another day.

George shared a room with six others. By now some airmen had built temporary beds by nailing old boards to two-by-four supports against the wall. It took George a while to find sleep that night. In his mind, he had created a liftoff with him aboard. He imagined the flight between the clouds and flying over the Adriatic Sea. He fell asleep with the feeling of freedom intact in his heart.

Images of barefoot people walking on soft grass visited his sleep that night. Natives of Yugoslavia appeared on the highest mountain summits. They were dancing the circular dance of freedom. The sky was clear and deep blue. The natives signaled him to join their dance. Clarinet sounds waving in the air, hands clapping and shouts of joy. Suddenly the sky darkened - A flock of giant black birds flew overhead, so close he could touch them. Thunder and lightning shook the sky. Voices from behind him urged him to run. The voices sounded surreal.

"Let's go! Let's go! Move out!"

He jumped off his board bed and began to run to the stairs. By the time he hit the bottom of the stairs, he was wide awake and aware of what was happening. Bombs were falling. The concussion from one bomb blew him backward onto the stairs. Tiles from the roof rained down on him. He stood up and ran barefoot over the broken tile. In a few seconds, George was outside and found himself among several running men. He went over a four-foot fence without touching the wire. He was in mid-air when the third bomb exploded. George fell into a trench with shrapnel and dirt flying around him. More bodies fell into the trench. He looked up to the sky. A Junkers JU88 twin-engine combat aircraft was dropping bombs on them. The German bomber made a slow turn, came back over the same path, and dropped three more five hundred-pound bombs. One of the bombs fell on their building. People were still running for safety. He checked to see if those around him were okay as the enemy plane picked up speed and disappeared far into the horizon. None of them were injured. The ones who were not able to make it to the trench suffered shrapnel wounds. But, everyone was alive.

George went back to their building to check the damage. Everything was covered in debris and stones. Their bedroom now matched all the rest of the town's buildings: it had no roof. When night fell, they marched back to the airfield. The sky was once again entirely covered by clouds. A ray of hope made his heart beat in anticipation of flying away from here. He heard the engines and then he saw the red flare shooting up to the sky. The ray of hope would have to wait for tomorrow. They returned to their open-roof housing, to wait for one more day. Manny Cardenas was telling his story of how he escaped the onslaught of the valley of death, a few days back. But what he did not know was that Shaun O'Brien was hiding in a ditch near him. The Germans were walking in the valley below not far from him and O'Brien had to be quiet. He was also hit on his right hip by shrapnel during the onslaught of flying bullets and his leg felt numb. He could not run fast enough without being detected by the Germans. He watched the entire ordeal of the Germans checking everybody to confirm they were dead. O'Brien was surprised that the Germans gave medical care to the few injured, among them was Andy Ryker who could not stand on his feet and was carried out on a stretcher. Bill Stoney's body was left behind.

Trails of Tragedy and Triumph

19

ANOTHER WORLD

And so, they came to a strange and unfriendly country, by the hundreds of thousands, young and old to find gold on the streets. Only to discover they were here to do the jobs that nobody else wanted to do and to be regarded as inferior and stupid.

Adjusting to this new society was difficult, but most of them held their head high, did the dirty work, learned English, bought their own homes and started their own businesses. Their children and grandchildren fought in wars clad in American uniforms, became leaders in politics, wealthy businesspeople, doctors, lawyers, intellectuals and great athletes.

They never wanted to hide their foreignness – they were proud of their roots. In fact, the opposite, they created little ethnic cities within the city and spread their culture, food and music into the mainstream population.

Starting a new life with no job experience and without speaking the language seemed like an impossible task. But the human spirit excels when facing the impossible. If there were members of the family or friends living in the United States, they would help them get a place to stay and find work. For the rest, they had to find their way. The jobs available for them were unskilled work; building roads, washing dishes, cleaning sewers and streets. Women usually worked as seamstresses in the garment industry or their homes.

The first families of immigrants clustered in industrial cities, where there was a greater need for cheap labor. They stayed in neighborhoods where they could find affordable housing. In these neighborhoods they installed their culture's identity, some of them established small businesses to satisfy the needs of fellow immigrants. Their neighborhood streets reflected ethnic games, music, dancing. There were food vendors and people selling fruit from the pushcarts. The initial isolation in their ethnic ways created an incredible bond within the family, closeness with the community and kept them connected with their country's roots. One of these communities was Astoria in New York City.

Yiannis and Eleni Yiannopoulos immigrated to America in the early nineteen-hundreds, when Eleni was pregnant with Giorgos. When they start working their names changed to John and Helen Poulos and baby George because the American tongue was overwhelmed with their given names. They made their home in Astoria.

Most of the Greek immigrants settled at first in large urban centers, mainly in Boston, New York, Chicago and Los Angeles. Eventually they scattered across America into many smaller cities, where they built their communities with a strong ethnic presence. Throughout the years, Astoria became a home away from home for Greeks. Living in Astoria did not feel like living in the United States, it was as if they were in a Greek city. Everything in Astoria was Greek; the language, grocery stores, restaurants, bakeries and nightclubs. Even Greek banks are there. And of course, there are churches, Greek schools and parades for the Greek independence days. Astoria is a town in Queens, bounded by the East River, and near Manhattan and Brooklyn. Thousands of visitors take the time to cross over and get a taste of Greece. For the Greeks, Astoria was the place of their roots. For the visitors it is where they can have fun experiencing the Greek culture. It is like being in Athens, the only thing missing is the hill of Acropolis.

George and Helen Poulos had three more children, a boy and two girls. They saved enough money to open a small grocery shop in Astoria. They sold Mediterranean products, and of course, decorated it with Greek flags and posters of the Acropolis and Santorini. The family's business grew and expanded their services by delivering Mediterranean food to nearby restaurants. By the end of the ninety-twenties, their truck was supplying most of the local restaurants. After World War II, as more Greeks migrated to the United States and Mediterranean foods were introduced to the general population, their wholesale business became a major food supplier.

Despite coming to America from mostly poor backgrounds, Greek immigrants moved rapidly into entrepreneurs. By the end of the nineteen-twenties, Greeks were operating over twenty-five thousand businesses, such as restaurants, candy shops, ice cream manufacturers and florists in New York City and Chicago alone.

Trails of Tragedy and Triumph

20

THE WANDERERS

It was past midnight. The excitement of freedom was mounting inside John Mueller. Men were sleeping peacefully all around him, yet he could only toss and turn, trying to keep his eyes closed. Eventually, he gave up trying to sleep and got up.

He walked outside. Small groups of airmen sat around; some were enjoying a cigarette, others were seated wrapped in their thoughts. Mueller felt a strange bonding with these airmen; the feeling of camaraderie was strong. There was no question that they would sacrifice their lives for one another. The exchange of words between them was limited as if they were afraid to know one another too closely. The possibility of death was existing on every step and at any time. Most of these men had learned to maintain a safe distance as if the pain of the loss of a stranger would be less severe than the loss of a close friend. But the bond between them was strong and undeniable.

saThey were a family of wanderers in a strange land and, against all the odds, they had survived.

In the still of the night, there was a sound of plane engines. Mueller's first instinct was to run for cover, but he remained standing as he observed the others sitting, unmoved as if they knew that the approaching aircraft was a welcoming sound. The outline of a C46 transport plane appeared from behind the mountains. The pilot lowered his aircraft between the mountaintops and dropped a few packages. Then he lifted the nose of the plane over the mountains and flew away. What was dropped on the small field was not bombs but food.

This act doubled Mueller's certitude that he was relatively safe here and now. A team of airmen hiked down the hill to pick up the packages.

When dawn broke, he was still awake. He waited for the first meal at midmorning with great anticipation. After that he went to his room and lay in his spot, enjoying the contentment of a full stomach.

He reminisced about his childhood, trying to collect his thoughts and understand what gave him the strength to endure such an adventure. He thought about the times he spent with his best friend, Bill. His eyes teared when thinking of him.

Growing up in Michigan had been hard for John and Bill, but not much different from other poor kids around the country. They scrounged for nickels, they worked long and hard for very little, and they took pleasure in small victories. John smiled at the picture in his mind of selling shells and corn cobs with his friend. He could almost feel the wind blowing through his hair as he drove his Chevy around town. Life had not always been kind, but he had learned to work hard. He had learned to be resourceful and keep on working, even when he was tired and would rather be playing. Above all, it seemed his life had been about changes, always moving around, always going to new schools and meeting new people and always finding ways to earn a living. Not a bad education, he thought, for a guy who ended up having to count on pure endurance for survival. John Mueller had always struggled to find ways to pull some meaning from the losses and hardships he had been dealt. This trip which started with being shot down to finally coming back to safety had been no different.

When Mueller closed his eyes, moving pictures ran through his mind. He remembered the streets that he ran through with his best friend, Bill. The footsteps of their little feet were urgently trying to get to the local milling company. They wanted to get there before the other kids so that they could collect bags full of corncobs from the cob-bin. Several other poor kids, most of them barefooted, ran to the cob-bin with their bags. Once there, there was a race of filling as many bags possible and as much as they could carry. The two friends sold the corncobs to the businesses around town that used them as kindling to start fires since everyone in town had a coal stove or furnace.

They would pay ten cents a bag in the wintertime and five cents in the summer.

The two boys were partners in other jobs, as well. In the bowling alley, they would set up the pins on the four lanes. They worked until midnight and got paid two cents a lane and occasionally would pick up a quarter thrown down the alley by a wealthy bowler. That is where the two boys got a lot of exercise because they had to hurry and pick up all the downed pins and clear the alley before the next ball came. The jump-run-pick-get-out-of-the-way process continued for hours.

They also started picking clam from the clear waters of the river. That was a skillful job. The clams or mussels buried themselves in the riverbed. The only part they could see through the glass of their peeker box was their feelers waving in the moving water. The peeker box was made out of a wood frame about one-foot square with a glass bottom.

Their fishing tool was a three-foot-long rod with a flattened end; it looked just like a golf club. When the boys spotted the mussels' antennas waving, they quickly inserted the flat end of the poker-rod into the opening of the mussel. Under the impact of the rod, the shellfish closed, trapping the poker inside its shell. Then they pulled it up from the river bottom and deposited it in a floating tub that was tied around their waist.

When the tub was filled, they floated it back to their campsite where a cooker was set up. The cooker was a container placed on cement blocks. When they had filled the cooker, the boys added water and started a fire under it. For the fire, they used old cut up tires. They covered the mussels with burlap sacks to hold them steady. After the mussels had been fully steamed and opened up, the mussels were shoveled out onto a makeshift sorting table.

The two partners extracted the meat and fed it to the fish. The shells were sorted out into number one and number two qualities and placed in burlap bags. The shell buyers for the button factory paid three cents per pound for the good ones and one cent per pound for the number two shells. John and Bill got to watch once as the workers dumped loads of shells into big aluminum tanks in the basement of the factory. When the shells were soft, big machines cut button blanks by the thousands. Then they were shipped off to different factories where buttons were used. The two boys spent entire summers shelling on the river.

In their spare time, the two partners went around picking up aluminum, brass, copper and iron items from trash cans. They sold them to the junkyard, where old Joe, the junk-man paid a few cents per pound. The price varied depending on the metal.

Those years the two boys spent the least amount of time

possible at home. The two practically grew up on their own, as did many kids their age during those difficult years. There were people like old Joe the junk dealer who cared about them and even gave them some work on Saturdays. He trusted them to weigh junk, paper and cardboard that other kids brought in. There was also Mister Harvey, the small candy store owner who felt sorry for them and would say, "come over here kids." and hand them candy.

 He remembers when they were sixteen years old, they both got their driver's license. There were now men, and a man needs a car. Bill Stoney could care less about having a car, but John Mueller was determined to get one. Between the two of them, they saved twenty dollars and bought a two-door 1926 Chevrolet. John said that this dark green Chevrolet was the most beautiful thing in the whole world. With enormous excitement the two boys drove the car out of the lot. John felt like he was flying between soft white clouds.

Trails of Tragedy and Triumph

21

LIFT OFF

Dark clouds remained stubbornly in the sky, preventing their departure. George Poulos fell asleep trusting that the next day the air will be clear. But the next night the heavy clouds remained in the sky.

With a heavy heart, the airmen made their trek to the airfield anyway. Thirty-three airmen stood quietly at the end of the airfield, expecting the same routine: the engine drone, the red flare, and the long walk back. George heard the plane's engines and he sensed the excitement of everyone around him. Looking up at the sky, he observed the clouds standing graceless and stubborn. The roar of the engines grew louder.

His eyes were glued to the sky.

Suddenly he noticed a small opening. The clouds seemed to part and open like curtains to reveal the gray sky. By the time the aircraft was above them, the opening between the clouds was about one hundred yards wide.

George held his breath, thinking that the moment of redemption had arrived.

"A miracle," someone whispered.

George watched their commander lift his gun to shoot the flare. The lifting of his hand toward the sky seemed to be in slow motion. George's eyes followed the barrel of the gun. Finally, the flare came out - It was green and bright. Green was the color of freedom now.

In a few seconds, the C46 came through the opening of the clouds at a very steep angle. The pilot leveled off the plane inside the mountain range, made a circle, and pointed its nose down for a landing. He taxied to the end of the field with the door open. The crew chief on the plane was throwing out supplies while the plane was moving, and the team of airmen who had escorted them down to the field was retrieving the boxes and crates.

"Let's go, go, go! Move, move, move!" the colonel urged the men to get on the plane.

They needed no urging. All of them were off and running. It took about three minutes for all of them to jump on board. Then the pilot gave it full power and headed directly at a cliff.

With every second that passed, the cliff was coming closer. George held his breath and they all held onto one another preparing for a crash. They were just a few yards away from the cliff when the pilot pulled the nose of his plane up sharply. The overloaded plane creaked as it labored upward. Just as he was thinking of the possibility of the plane breaking down, there was a loud crash on the left side of the plane. A rush of cold air filled the plane.

"Hold on," voices cautioned. They did just that, holding on to anything they could find.

Under the extreme strain on the fuselage, the cargo door had opened. The pressure of the wind broke it off and blew it away. Over the commotion of unbalanced bodies, George saw the plane barely clearing the cliff. The pilot circled inside the mountain range and then the plane was wrapped in the clouds. But they were not out of danger yet.

The pilot pulled the nose of the aircraft up, undertaking the difficult and uncertain task of clearing the mountaintops. George knew that every second the plane held its nose up there was a possibility of a crash. They all sat helplessly, directing their faith and prayers towards the pilot.

Suddenly the plane leveled off and headed west. At first, George let out a sigh of relief, and then he was overcome with admiration for the pilot. Without question, this was the most skillful piloting he had ever witnessed.

Soon they left the heavy clouds behind them, but their situation was still dangerous. The pilot had to fly at a low altitude to avoid detection by German radar. This was a cargo plane; it was not equipped for combat.

When they finally sighted the Adriatic Sea, they broke out into wild cheers - they were well on their way to freedom. Everyone turned to thank the crew of the cargo plane. It was only then that he noticed familiar faces.

This was the same crew that had flown the crew of Lucky Lady from Casablanca to Manduria, Italy when they were on their way to report for duty.

It was the same pilot who had impressed George back then when they made a stop to pick up a load of ammunition. To land, he had to touch the ground, fly over dip in the runway, touch ground again, fly over another dip, and then finally set it down. After loading the ammunition, the pilot turned the aircraft back to the dirt runway and, through landings and flying over dips, lifted the plane back up into the sky. That experience was the most exciting landing and takeoff that George had witnessed in his young flying career. Now the same pilot was flying the surviving airmen to Italy, after another unforgettable takeoff.

Trails of Tragedy and Triumph

22

DELIVERANCE

The drunkenness of freedom ran high in their veins during the flight from Yugoslavia to Italy. They were all anxious to step onto friendly soil - every moment of the flight seemed endless. When the plane's tires finally, touched the ground and the bumps of the landing were felt, there was quietness, as if this was an improbable moment. Soon after there were ecstatic reactions, shouting, rejoicing and embracing. As the plane reduced speed and rolled off the runway onto the tarmac, airmen on the ground waved on the plane, welcoming home its passengers. John Mueller looked outside, the airmen welcoming them home had clean uniforms and new shoes. John still wore his flight suit, soiled and ripped, with the legs cut off. He looked at his military boots and thought of the rebel Goran who gave him these shoes – God bless him. John had not shaved or bathed for many days and he felt as if he was coming back from time travel, returning from land that existed long ago.

As he stepped down from the plane and experienced the sounds, the energy of the airport and the vehicles driving around, he felt for a moment that he was observing a distant world. The plane that lifted the airmen to freedom landed in Bari, Italy. It was surreal to hear people speaking a familiar language. There were jeeps and trucks everywhere. The sounds and commotion of the airport had replaced the quietness of the mountains.

Among the vehicles, there were several ambulances ready to take the newcomers directly to the hospital, where they were housed in secure section. First, they had to get rid of the lice through a delousing steam bath. Their first shower for over a month was one of the most enjoyable aspects of this rediscovered civilization. At the shower exit, they were given hospital gowns and then taken to the emergency rooms for treatment. Those who were injured were hospitalized. The rest of them were taken into the mess hall for coffee, milk and donuts. There were more surprises besides the seductive aroma of coffee and the smell of donuts. There were tables and chairs, glasses and plates. And while anticipating the mouthwatering treats, everyone slowly realized that it was true; they were free! What a glorious feeling that was. The monumental events of the recent past suddenly seemed like a bad dream, a dream that they knew was true and one that they would never forget.

After coffee and donuts, with happy stomachs they were shown to guarded tents. These tents were set up in a secluded area of the hospital grounds. John Mueller lay down slowly on his army cot. He had not slept on a bed for many nights. When the clean sheets wrapped around his clean body, he felt a sweet embrace that brought a smile to his face. He closed his eyes and envisioned the land that he had left behind. There were endless miles; how many miles exactly, he did not know. There were endless mountaintops he had to climb, peaks that, at the time, were obstacles to his freedom. However, now he could look back and remember the beauty, the green trees, the currents of clear water, the wild birds, and the rugged countryside. He remembered the valleys that he had to cross, devastated by man's incompetence to communicate and get along with his fellow man. Now, he could see the green grass, the daisies, and the poppies that he had left behind. He remembered the deep blue skies of the night that were embroidered with a myriad of stars. He could feel the crisp air on the mountaintops. John Mueller could not forget the kind faces of the wonderful folks who generously shared with him the little they had. It was that little bit that kept him alive and gave him the strength to walk farther. He had made a conscious decision to embrace the beauty of life and let the pain remain a ghost of the past.

In their secluded area they were given strict orders not to discuss their activities of the past month with anyone and were told that they would be in isolation until their individual debriefing. During the debriefing, the officers first congratulated them and expressed great admiration for the fact that they had survived the wilderness and the enemy. They then wanted to know all the details of their mission, how they got shot down and what they had seen. The officers took some notes on everyone's account of the long march and about the rebels who had protected and guided the Americans to safety. At the end, the officers stressed the great importance of disclosing nothing to anyone about their rescue, or about the details of the ordeal they experienced in enemy territory.

The three officers in charge took turns to express the importance of secrecy.

"The safety of hundreds of airmen depends on the secrets of the airfield and the method of retrieval."

"Revealing any details about your rescue will result in a court-martial."

"It is only when you will be notified in writing, that you will be able to discuss your experiences. Until such a letter arrives in your hand, you are under a gag order."

After debriefing, they were given new uniforms. Mueller's uniform was much smaller than the one he had when leaving for the mission to Steyr. When John Mueller had his khakis on, tears clouded his eyes as he realized what a great honor it was to serve his country. That moment was one of the proudest moments of his life.

After a few days, Art Bauer, Bob Pastorelli, Clark Bailey, and Manny Cardenas arrived in Bari to go through their debriefing After that, the six members of Lucky Lady were sent back to their base in Lecce. Their arrival at the base turned out to be a great welcoming event. Everyone looked at them as if they saw ghosts. It turned out that during their last bombing mission, a war correspondent was flying on the plane next to Lucky Lady. He had reported that Lucky Lady had lost a wing and crashed into the mountainside with all of the crew inside. Six of Lucky Lady's crew was back to safety, but their minds were with the other four that were missing.

23

PROUD MOMENTS

From where Shaun O'Brien was hiding he saw the Germans go around the valley of death checking for survivors, making sure that all the people laying on the ground were dead. The German soldiers picked up four children and three women and escorted them back to the village. Two other soldiers lifted Andy Ryker from the ground; his legs shot, unable to even stand. They brought a gurney and he too was taken to the village. The rest of the German soldiers followed, leaving dead bodies behind, including Bill Stoney.

When the Germans occupied the valley of death and the village, it seemed that they were there to stay. Shaun O'Brien stayed hidden in his ditch until nightfall before attempting to escape the German's well-guarded land. Shortly after the German's cleared out, he walked slowly and with occasional stops. O'Brien escaped into a narrow cave about a mile away from the valley. He was disturbed by what he had seen and wanted time to deal with his anxiety. He rested for a while before getting up and moving, now with faster steps. Using his sense of directions, O'Brien moved southbound.

He survived by eating greens from the forest for two days. The third morning, exhausted, thirsty and dizzy, his body dropped on a mountain slope and fell into darkness. In the midst of the fogginess of his lethargic stage, he noticed movements. Soon he realized that he was being carried on a makeshift stretcher by two men. "Where am I?" He reacted. "Okay, okay, good." the third man walking by his stretcher trying to calm him. A short time later they reached a small village. The rebels who carried him were trying to explain that he was to stay there until he was better. They tried to explain that three days from now another team of rebels will pick him up and bring him to the secret airfield. The Natives took him in, fed him and took care of him. He waited until the next group of rebels came by the village and followed them on the route to freedom. Shaun O'Brien had made many friends in the village. Saying goodbye to them was an emotional experience. Once he reached the secret airport he was lifted back to his base in Lecce. He was greeted by his crew-mates who were anxious to hear the news. There were all there except Chris Moody, Andy Ryker and Bill Stoney.

"I do not know what happened to Chris. I stayed hidden and watched as the Germans were cleaning up the valley full of bodies. Andy was injured. He couldn't even stand on his feet. The Germans carried him off with a stretcher." He paused for a moment. "And Bill." he tried to continue, but his voice trembled. He sat down unable to look at his friends. "I am sorry, I am sorry." He broke down. John Mueller legs gave in, he threw himself on a chair and stared into space.

He will never see his best friend again.

The second day after they all arrived at the base, the commander called the surviving crew of seven. He had ordered a small parade in their honor, and he asked all of them to stand beside him.

As the airmen marched past the seven heroes, there was

an overwhelming sense of pride, relief for returning home and sadness for their lost friends. They stood erect across from the American flag that waved steadily in the breeze. When the commander gave the "eyes right" in salute, to the marching soldiers, there were massive waves of chills and chests swelled with a great feeling of honor. Tears rolled down their cheeks. The returning soldiers raised their arms to return the salute. A small band played the National Anthem as the base commander stood in front of each of them and decorated their uniforms with various medals. He then saluted with pride and congratulated all of them.

The next day they boarded a flight back to the United States. None of them would be allowed back into the European Theater of War. German Intelligence had their names and if they happened to be shot down again anywhere in Europe and caught by the Germans, they would be considered spies and executed.

During their trip back to the States, they all were in deep thoughts. John Mueller's mind tried to recall the memories with his friend – memories which he will forever hold close to his heart. John's mind traveled back to the times before his military years, when he was trying to make some sense of his life and to understand the people whom he addressed as family members. There was not much ground for respect. His parents were two people who were caught up in their struggles in life. For John's childhood perspective, they were two people who gave him birth, hard times and worries. That was all.

While he was lying back on the seat of the plane, John smiled as he reminisced about his adolescent years. The only person who was always by his side was his friend Bill. Now he was gone.

Along the river, where they grew up, there were several stores. One of them, a drug store with an ice cream soda fountain, was a favorite spot for all the town's kids. It was where he and Bill use to hang out. The owner, a kind Italian man, had a five-cent Sunday for the poor kids who never had a dime. Everyone else paid the dime. John will always have a warm spot in his heart for Mr. Greco, the owner of the shop who was always kind to him and Bill.

During the short time when John lived with the Stoney family, he felt that he was finally in a healthy environment to raise a child. Bill's parents made him feel like he had a family. School was fun because he was in the same school as Bill, and he was surrounded with plenty of other children. His heart saddened as he thought of Bill's parents when they hear the news about their son. John did not want to leave the Stoney's house. He begged his mother to let him stay, but she wouldn't listen and his mother was his legal guardian, so he had to go.

As his mother's new boyfriend drove the Model T Ford Coupe away, John looked back from the window, watching Bill wave goodbye until a far turn took him away from his friend – John wasn't sure where they were going. On the way to wherever they were going, they had to go up some long hills. On one of the hills, the car's engine stopped - the car was out of gas. Oh, great, John thought this guy doesn't have money for gas. Actually, the problem was that the Model T had the gas tank under the seat, and as a result, the engine is higher than the gas tank. Consequently, the gas did not keep the carburetor full going up long hills. His mother had the idea to let the car coast down the hill backwards until the gas tank and the engine was level. Then they would restart the engine and turn the car around, backing up all the way to the top of the hill. Of course, if the gas tank was full with gas, this would not have been a problem. John's fears were true, this guy named Ross, never had enough money to buy food, never mind a luxury item such as a full tank of gasoline.

He came to dislike steep hills, mainly because of this ordeal. Hills meant trouble.

Rivers were a different story because they offered good fishing, and that was his favorite pastime as a kid. He would always go with his friend Bill and they would often catch game fish and sell them to various customers.

He remembers one day when they were twelve years old; they were fishing off a bridge in the center of town when Bill spotted a huge black bass. The water was clear, and about twelve feet deep. John let the bait go with the current and past the fish's nose. When the fish ignored it, John moved it over a little and placed it in front of his nose again. The fish did not appear to be hungry, but after the bait had hit his nose half-a-dozen times, he lost his temper and snapped it. John had a difficult time landing him but finally pulled him over the bridge rail and onto the sidewalk. Several people had gathered around to watch the two kids catch the big fish. A man came out from the crowd and asked for their names. After they told him, he took a ruler from his coat pocket to measure their bass. It was twenty- four inches long! The man then told them that he was a game warden. The boys got scared since they had no permit for fishing, and they thought that they were going to jail for sure. But they were relieved when the warden said that he was going to send their names and a story about their catch to a sports magazine. The boys sold the big bass to one of their customers for one dollar and fifty cents. Usually, they got twenty-five cents for their catch.

When they were teenagers, John and Bill worked in a junkyard. Someone drove an old 1926 Model T Ford into the yard one day to sell it for junk. The two boys wanted to buy it, and old Jack, the owner of the junkyard, let them take it for a test drive. A few blocks away the uphill slope was too much for the old car. It began to back down the hill. John, who was driving the car, saw the sheriff's car coming up over the top of the hill. He knew he was in trouble and let off the brakes and the car rolled backward at full speed and eventually became out of control, running off the dirt road.

The boys were trapped between two disparate elements, trying to bring the car under control and fleeing to escape the sheriff. Usually, when you are desperate, things turn to drama or comedy or both.

As the car went off the road and the rear axle hit a big rock, the right wheel was lifted off the ground and John was thrown out of the car. He was lying on his stomach, when Bill went full force on the dashboard. When John finally lifted his head, he was faced with the sheriff's boots. Slowly he lifted his eyes, afraid to see the expression on the sheriff's face. The sheriff gave the boys a scare at first and then a lecture for not having a driver's licenses or plates and let them go saying, "Take this damned junk heap back to old Jack. And don't let me catch you driving again." But the seduction of driving your first car is overwhelming. So, John and Bill did sneak in a few drives around the junkyard. Eventually, the car broke down and good-old Jack gave the boys their money back.

Bill was bigger and stronger than the other kids in school. He took it upon himself to protect John from the bullies. John loved cars. For a while, he worked for a car dealer, to clean parts and run errands making a dollar a day. His mother was on her second marriage to a guy named Phil. John's new stepfather would scream obscenities at his mother and if John ever tried to defend her, Phil became extremely angry. As John grew older, he felt that now was the time to stand up and protect his mother.

One day John surprised Phil. During one of his temper tantrums, John grabbed Phil's neck and slammed him to the floor.

"That's enough! Don't you ever raise your voice at my mother again," he said, pointing his fist right in Phil's face.

From that day on things changed around the house. Phil became less abusive and John's mother became more confident. She filed for a divorce and Phil went on his way. John's father showed up from time to time to visit, but he was married to a woman with three children and was living his own life. About a year later John's mom met David and married him. David treated his mother with love and respect.

The two boys continued to work together when possible and hang out at the movie theater every Tuesday. During the Great Depression the movie theaters, to bolster attendance, would future a game called Screeno. It was a form of bingo on the screen, in which the audiences had a chance to win cash.

One Tuesday night John hit the jackpot. The payoff was sixty-five dollars. The boys bought new clothes and had a real treat – pizza and coke. Besides working in the bowling alley setting up pins, they also went to work for Edie, who owned the local pool hall.

In the back of the hall, serious poker games thrived at night. Gambling was illegal, but no one ever bothered them.

John's job was to rake a quarter from every pot for the house and Bill's was to change the deck of cards for a new one every so often. Of course they also cleaned up the place after the games. During the day the two boys practiced on the pool table until they were good enough to play for the house against any player who came willingly to bet for a game of pool. Eventually, Edie sold the pool hall and they were out of work.

John joined the Civilian Conservation Corps and was sent to Wisconsin, where dams were being built. He sent some of his money to his mother. He was her only source of support after her husband died. During the wintertime working out in the cold became unbearable, so John left the bitter winter behind and started back home to Michigan.

John was shy with the girls – Bill, on the other hand, was popular because of his good looks and personality. On a blind date, Bill introduced Paula to John. Paula was the best friend of Diana, Bill's Fiancée.

The four of them went on double dates often.

Soon after that, the boys went to work for the Works Progress Administration, another government project. They were fortunate to get a job close to their home where a new bridge was to be built across the river in front of the stores, as well as a complete new dam in the same location. By now Bill had married Diana in a simple ceremony, and John was engaged to Paula.

They both were looking forward to working hard, saving money and starting families. This job would mean work for several years. It was there that Bill had the accident that severely burned his leg. It was there that their life changed when they heard the news about the Pearl Harbor tragedy.

John's thoughts were interrupted as the plane landed on American soil, in New Jersey.

24

CIVILIZED

The ending of the spring was approaching, the soil was moist with dewdrops and fragrance emanated from the citrus trees. A gentle breeze blew and filled Moody's heart with a refreshing dew. Beyond the green paradise, there was a ruthless world shadowed by man's primitive need to kill, to destroy. It was an image of tenderness and strength. Over the small dirt-yard, sweet grapes were hanging from the canopy of grapevines. Occasionally, Chris Moody would hear a distant noise from beyond the vast blue sky. He imagined airplanes flying, searching for targets. Behind him there were the countless miles of earth he had walked on; from the high peaks and foothills to the deep rocky canyons, valleys. He had walked from the ridges which dropped into the broad gravelly slopes of the mountains to the intimidating distant landscape, before getting to the next mountain.

"I can't wait to get back to civilization." He had heard some of his friends saying during their walk, but all he could think about was the kindness of the elderly couple who was taking care of him. Are they not civilized? Just because they do not have a telephone, a radio or a hair blower; are they barbarians? – Come on now. Petar and Marija were the kindest people he had ever met. If that is not civilized - what is?

This small community of eleven homes was nested in a small patch of land, enclosed by tall mountains that served as their fortress. All of the residents were older couples. It was as if this was an old person's retreat – they were left alone. They grew vegetables in their gardens, ate fruit from the citrus trees, milked their goats and they seemed content. They shared what they had. Chris and his keepers did not speak a word of the each-others language, but they had no problem getting along and managed to communicate just fine. When he showed them a photograph of his fiancée, Marija said *"Veoma lepa!"* (very beautiful) She smiled and touched the picture gently as if she wanted to give her a blessing. Petar tapped Chris's back, knotted his head and approved with an open hearted smile.

Occasionally Chris climbed the summit of the shorter mountain to find out if there was life beyond this forgotten village, but all he saw was the view of the surrounding steep canyons and mountains stretching outwards hundreds of miles; a breathtaking panorama of rugged topography.

As the light morning breeze caressed his face, he recalled his childhood on his father's ranch; Wearing his cowboy hat, white shirt, cowboy boots, and Levi's. Chris Moody grew up on his father's ranch in Northeastern Arizona, where the stars at night sparkle like jewels on a dark indigo blanket. There were thousands of acres of orchards, bushes of chaparral and wild desert grasslands. There were meadows carpeted with desert marigold, creosote bushes and blossoms of yellow, purple and red. The land spread out to rolling hills covered with lush greenery and desert wildflowers. At a young age, Chris enjoyed riding around the ranch on his father's horse, galloping between the sheep and cattle roaming the ranch and watching the workers picking potatoes and beans or doing other chores. The work on the ranch was never-ending. His father took his son hunting, to watch rodeos and tried to teach him how to brand livestock. In the Spring, the workers branded new cattle and leveled the ground for seeding. They moved cattle from pasture to pasture more often and made any necessary repairs in the summer. In the fall they repaired the farm equipment, buildings and chopped firewood. And in the winter they had to feed the cattle and livestock every day since the pastures were usually frozen. As Chris grew older, he was obligated to learn how to do all these chores. He was the only son and eventually would take over running the ranch. Chris felt that it wasn't exciting mending fences and chopping wood for the bunkhouse stoves and fireplaces nor was he happy to milk the cows every morning and night and collect eggs from the chickens.

Additionally, Chris Moody did not agree with the way his father treated the help. The people of his inner circle would drink whiskey and eat steak, baked potatoes and pies in the main dining room, while the lower help would eat corn, baked beans and water- based potato soup, sitting in the stables or their crowded rooms. His father, was a tall, lean cowboy with an intimidating presence. He would treat the low paid workers with contempt and his cowboy friends with smiles. One of the most challenging times of his life was when Chris had to tell his father that he did not want to be a rancher.

Chris Moody was an adventurer. He loved traveling, sports and parties. The ranch was a short drive from Flagstaff and Chris would sneak away with the red pick-up Chevy truck and drive on route 66 to Flagstaff to meet his friends. On his trips to Flagstaff, Chris would always buy some treats like crackers and chips for the adult low paid workers, and candy bars for their children. U.S. Route 66 brought thousands into Flagstaff as it was the main road to bring fruits and vegetables from California to Northern Arizona. Flagstaff was also the ideal location to rest for travelers going west from the mid-western states, and a major stop for the east-west transcontinental railroad destined for Chicago and Los Angeles. Towards the end of the nineteen-thirties, along this voguish route, there were numerous saloons, motels, gas stations, and restaurants. For young Chris and his friends, there was plenty of entertainment and activities, and an ideal place to meet girls.

The first night Chris Moody spent with the elderly couple in the forgotten village was a restless night. There was a peculiar excitement sleeping on a real bed and he was still concerned about his safety. Maybe it was a reaction to the past few days and the fact that he was not used to this kind of hospitality. Even though the exhaustion from the day's events was overwhelming, the images of the dead in the valley of death, weighed heavily on his mind.

The first day in the village was newsworthy for the residents. Petar and Marija walked with Chris around the two narrow streets, introducing him to the neighbors. Everyone smiled and welcomed him as if he was their long, lost son. On the second night, his eyelids could not stay open, his sleep was so peaceful, he even was able to have a dream. His body went to sleep but his mind refused to rest, taking him to strange places. There was an enormous wave lifting him up and tossed him onto another wave. Down the wide river, he was carried by the waves. The river water was brown and the waves were intense. The river was running in the middle of the deserted land, surrounded by brown hills and trees black in the aftermath of a great fire. Up and down the waves carried him. Suddenly an odd calmness overtook him, letting the rolling waves command his body to whatever destination until abruptly, he was lying by the riverside. The sun was hot, drying his wet clothes, warming his skin. He stood up, his face unshaven and barefooted, his lips chapped from thirst and his clothes ripped to shreds. Ahead of him towered a tall mountain. It was bare except for the very top where it had blossomed with greenery. Pretty birds flew around the trees on top of the mountain, singing cheerfully. He began to walk toward the top of the mountain. He was sure he could find water up there and fruit to eat. He was almost at the top when his legs gave out, and he began to back down. Faster and faster he walked backward, until he was at the foot of the mountain again, back where he started. He climbed again, determined to reach the top, only to back down again. On his way down two wrinkled hands held his hands, helping him up to the mountain. He looked at the faces; it was Petar and Marija smiling.

The next forty days in the remote village went on uneventfully. Chris's leg was about healed, and he had regained his strength. On the fortieth day two Partisan rebels showed up in the village, bringing medical supplies. They were greeted with the respect reserved for heroes. "*moj sin.*" (my son) said Petar, pointing to one of the men. Occasionally, Partisan rebels will bring medical supplies to remote places, like this one. After emotional and lengthy goodbyes from the villagers, Chris Moody walked along with the two men, heading up to the southwest mountain. He glanced back. The entire village population was standing at the edge of the village waving their handkerchiefs good-by. Chris waved back and placed his right hand over his heart, thanking them for saving his life. They walked and rested until the dawn.

Chris was asked to sit and wait. There was not much talking since the Partisans spoke no English. While waiting, he counted the rings carved on his cane; there were eighty-eight of them. A few hours had passed when a group of people appeared. There were three partisans walking in front of eight airmen. Chris followed them to reach the secret airfield eventually and from there to his base in Italy.

All the surviving members of Lucky Lady had reached Italy. After debriefing, he was put on a plane back to the United States. When the time came to report on his new assignment as an aerial gunner instructor at Harlingen, Texas. He learned that his new task was to fly in a B-24 bomber with students who were ready to practice firing fifty-caliber guns with live ammunition. On one of the missions with six of his students he noticed oil pouring out of engine number four as they were heading back to the base.

"We are losing oil from engine number four," Chris warned the pilot through the intercom. Of course, the pilot could see that the temperature was going up and that the oil pressure was dropping.

"I know, I know, we can fly on three engines," he replied.

Chris was concern that the engine would soon overheat and catch fire.

"You must get number four engine feathered before we lose all the oil," Chris warned the pilot. The pilot did not answer. Now Chris was concerned. The engineer's voice came through the intercom. "Don't call the pilot again; he's falling apart."

Chris did not like the tone of his voice. He seemed scared. Chris kept monitoring the ailing engine from his waist window, thinking – "here we go again."

They were approaching the base and, with a bit of luck, they might be able to land safely. Chris' concern was justified. He saw the first tongues of flames flicker out over the wing from number four engine.

"The engine is on fire," Chris warned the pilot. There was no answer.

"I repeat again the engine is on fire." There was silence from the cockpit.

He gathered his students to the top of the wings internal section where they would be safer in a crash. The aircraft lost its stability as they were coming in for a landing.

"Negative, you cannot land, one of your landing gears is not down," a voice said from the control tower. "You must go around again," the tower ordered their pilot. The voice came back from the tower, this time with urgency, "Your engine is on fire. Now, you must land." The pilot pulled the nose of the plane up but did not hit the engine throttles. The next thing Chris saw was the ground coming up to meet them. He was praying that this pilot could be skillful enough to avoid the crash, but that was a hopeless prayer. He braced himself as the plane dove into the stall. The nose hit the ground and the impact of the crash was tremendous. Bodies were thrown all around and aircraft parts shot up into the air.

"How ironic," Chris thought. He had survived the thick enemy flak; a plane shot down, the Germans and Chetniks. He survived the suffering of hunger, endless walking and terrible living conditions and legions of lice, only to end up dead in a crash in a cotton field in Texas during a training mission. But his lucky streak was still with him. Not only did he live but the impact of the crash buried the flaming engine enough in the soft ground to keep the fire contained.

Chris Moody urged the students to exit through the waist window. Then he went to the fuselage to get the fire extinguisher. He got out to the wing with the fire extinguisher to put out the last remnants of the engine fire. After the fire was out, he crawled under the badly crushed front of the plane and rushed to help the people trapped in the crumpled front of the fuselage. The pilot was frozen in his seat. His eyes and mouth were wide open. It was hard to say if he was dead or alive. The sirens sounded near. Soon the fire wagon, the big wrecker, and the ambulance arrived.

Miraculously, most of the people got out safely with only a few minor cuts and bruises. There were more people trapped under the top of the gun turret, up front.

"Are you okay?" the medic asked Moody.

It was then that he felt a sharp pain in his back and collapsed. The last thing he remembered was being loaded on a stretcher into the ambulance and the big wrecker boom trying to lift the top of the gun turret where some of the crew was trapped. When he came to he was in the hospital, he had suffered a fractured back and a concussion.

Chris Moody spent several days in the hospital. As for the pilot, he was later discharged from the service. It was determined, after a hearing, that he was not fit to fly under pressure. One month later Chris was back on flying status. On his first mission after the crash, everything went well except just before the landing. As they approached the runway, the number four engine suddenly quit. The pilot did everything he possibly could, but the landing was short of the runway. The plane hit the dirt and then the cement block, both main landing gear tires blew out, and they ended up dragging the tail down the runway. None of the crew was seriously injured. It was after that incident that the flight sergeant called Chris Moody to his office. He looked at him and shook his head in disbelief.

"You know, Moody, it's time for you to be grounded."

As much as Chris loved flying, he knew the sergeant was right. He was assigned to Base Intelligence where he was to teach gunnery students what to do to handle the situation of being shot down in enemy territory. For Chris teaching was routine. His fascination was with engines and with the dynamics of mechanisms. He could spend endless hours trying to figure out how things worked.

25

NEW LIFE

When Chris Moody was released from his military duty the Americans began to become heavily involved in the Korean War. Listening to the news reports about the war on the radio brought up a feeling of great nostalgia. Chris Moody was back in Flagstaff and living with his girlfriend. Chris and Susan had much in common; they both liked skiing, hiking and traveling. They talked about marriage and starting a family. But Chris knew that he wasn't ready to take on the great responsibility of husband and father. "I am not ready yet – if you wait for me I will be back to marry you – but I have to deal with my demons first!"

"And what are you going to do?" she asked.

"I am going to re-enlist."

Susan knew that the military was where he belonged.

"Whatever you think is best is fine with me," Susan said.

"The only bad thing about re-enlisting is that I'll be away for a while, but in the long run it will be better for us," he said.

Susan wrapped her arms around his neck. "I love you, Chris Moody," she said kissing him gently. "Let's get engaged before you go. Just so you know I will be waiting for you."

Moody's new specialty was teaching jet aircraft engine classes. In just a few months he was promoted to tech-sergeant and transferred to the F-84 and F-89 specialist course. The F-89 was a two-jet aircraft and extremely heavy. Since jet mechanics were very much in demand in the Korean War, he knew with his specialty he would probably go to Korea.

In February of 1951, Chris Moody was selected for reassignment in Korea.

Susan and Chris said their long good-byes. The last thing she said to him was, "Promise me that you will be careful."

The train took Chris Moody to California three days later. From the docks of San Francisco, he boarded a troop ship. The sleeping quarters on the ship were five-high tiers of hammocks. Chris was glad that he was in the highest tier because there was a crack in one of the ship's iron plates and it let water into the lower area. The water sloshed back and forth as the ship rocked and they hung their belongings off the floor to keep them dry.

The second day out on the open sea they ran into bad weather. Immense waves tilted the ship into a horizontal position and then swung it to the other side. The old vessel creaked under the strong waves. It was a frightening experience.

Every time a high wave knocked the ship to its side, Chris held his breath.

There were seasick people everywhere. You could hardly find an open toilet; even the sailors had their heads in the john. The intense rocking of the ship continued for two days. Nine days after surviving the high waves, the seasickness and the lousy food, they arrived in Japan. Military trucks took them from the port to an airfield. From there they flew to Korea.

At the airport in Korea, a jeep was waiting for him to take him to his maintenance squadron. Chris was surprised to see so much snow on the ground. He arrived on the field late at night and he was given an unused hut in the back of the barracks. Chris spent the night on a cot with a little stove to keep him warm. He set his cot up next to the stove, but it was impossible to keep warm. The snow outside had piled up over twelve inches and it was still snowing. He had never been so cold in his life.

He was glad to move into the barracks the next day. The work there was long and tiring. To keep up with the demands of the damaged planes, he worked fourteen hours a day, seven day a week.

The exact location of the squadron was unknown to the soldiers and their families. The primary planes on the base were the F-84s. The planes flew as many as four missions a day to support the efforts of the ground troops. Chris and Susan exchanged letters frequently and both were anxious to start their new life together. Chris often took Susan's picture out of his shirt pocket to look at her beautiful face, her green eyes and the auburn, long thick hair.

Two-and-a-half years after enlisting, the Korean War was over. Chris was anxious for the moment that he could hold Susan in his arms again. Their reunion was emotional. They both cried tears of joy. After their marriage, Chris continued to teach, and he became a successful motivational safety speaker, on topics such as overcoming adversity. On the living room wall in their home hung the hand-carved cane with eight-eight rings on it. He had carved the rings for each day he walked through the mountains and stayed in the village. It wasn't just there for sentimental reasons, but also to remind everyone the tragedy of war and the triumph of the human spirit - a spirit that touched his soul while staying with Petar and Marija in the small village. A painting reflecting the faces of Petar and Marija hung next to the cane.

When Bill Stoney introduced his friend John Mueller to Paula on their blind date, John Mueller felt emotions unknown to him. His heart pounded fast against his chest, his legs weakened, and a wave of uncustomary energy penetrated his entire being. On their first dinner date, after John's return from Europe, he wanted so badly to tell Paula every detail about his adventure in Yugoslavia. This was the first time that he wanted to impress someone by bragging about his unbelievable survival. With great difficulty, he kept the classified information to himself.

After dinner, he dropped Paula off at her place. When he escorted her to her door, John knew he was in love. Standing in front of her door, he said, "Someday I am going to marry you." Paula looked at him with eyes wide open from her apparent surprise at his statement. She began to laugh and said, "Oh, John, you don't even know me. This is only our second date."

The truth is that John surprised himself with his bold approach. But for the days to come, he was certain that Paula was the girl of his dreams. She was constantly on his mind, and all that mattered was their next date. Ten months after John came back from his adventure in Yugoslavia, Paula and John were married. They made their home in Fort Worth, Texas.

John was still tormented by the urge to reveal the details of his ordeal on the ground in Yugoslavia to Paula. Eventually, he learned to live with that urge. Paula and John enjoyed traveling with their twenty-five-foot glider house trailer. On one of their trips they visited Paula's sister, in Los Angeles. Paula's sister just had a baby. Paula and John spent most of their time admiring the three-month-old baby. This was the first time that he revealed a strong urge to have a child of his own.

On their way back to Fort Worth, John had an idea to build

a trailer park. They found a four-acre plot and bought it for one thousand dollars an acre. They began to build their trailer park.

John wanted to have a secure income before he started a family. He would never allow his child to experience the kind of childhood that he had.

It was in his trailer park that he received a letter from the government stating that enough time had passed and now he was free to talk about his experience in Yugoslavia. It was amazing how a generic letter on an inert piece of paper had activated memories and aroused emotions nested in the deep chambers of his memory. Long ago he had made a promise not to reveal the details that led to their survival. He kept his promise! He did not reveal the details even to the person he loved the most, the person who had become the other part of himself. Now he was free to talk about his amazing adventure. Paula looked at him with admiration. "Oh, John, the things that you went through," she said. John bowed his head. He was never comfortable receiving praise. "Well, I hope that it was worth it, that we were able to make a difference for the younger generation."

John believed that during the moments of warfare, a seed was planted in his mind, a seed that changed the meaning of his life. As his mind ranged over the history of the Great War, it was clear to him that the war, that any war, was not restricted to conflict between countries. It was the eternal struggle between good and evil. Most of those who witnessed the inhumane massacres and torture had those images hammering constantly in their minds. The very idea that they were part of the Great War added an immeasurable force behind their struggle for freedom. It was this force that has made their existence in this world bearable. Now that they have lived in the pages of history books and stood beside heroes with an indomitable spirit, they felt courage rising in their souls. The courage that blossomed from the seed of freedom.

The military service is never forgotten by anyone who experiences it. The elderly speak of it with unconcealed nostalgia, with the wistfulness one has a good experience. In some cases, the memory bears the nightmare of bullying and cruelty. The military is a mixture that contains multiple elements. The military offered the opportunity for a young man to experience rare feelings. John Mueller felt great satisfaction on his graduation day as an airplane mechanic. He had proud moments, one of which was his first day in school while marching in formation past the American flag. He experienced fascinating times in military school when he left not an inch of the airplane unexamined. He remembered the trails in the air depot, where there were no warplanes but twenty-mile hikes with full packs and gas masks. Unforgettable faces that he remembered with reverence. There were thrilling moments, like his first airplane ride at the gunnery school when he sat in the rear cockpit facing backward and he saw the ground drop away from the plane during takeoff. And it was destiny on Biggs Field, Texas, when he met the Lucky Lady's crew and then shared an unbelievable adventure. Together, after their advanced training in Tucson, Arizona, they went to California and boarded a ship to Casablanca. This was the same ship that, on its way back, was torpedoed and destroyed by the Germans.

In Casablanca, they stayed in an infantry tent city. That was the first time they experienced an unbelievable human tragedy. The war and subsequent poverty created a scene that broke everyone's heart. There were endless casualties, ruins everywhere; the whole population had turned into beggars. They had skin sores, diseases, deformities and many were missing an arm or a leg. It brought tears to their eyes. The food in their camp was inedible. Repeatedly the entire camp was under a roaring siege of diarrhea. Daytime was burning hot and nighttime was freezing cold.

They left the devastated people behind and were flown to Manduria, Italy. The picture of suffering and the smell of death remained intact in their mind. From Manduria they found their way to Lecce, Italy. However, nothing compared to the feeling he experienced when John had to tell Bill Moody's parents about their son's death. Although he remained calm on the outside, inside, there was an unbelievable pain, a pain that he had to eventually contend with but never forget. Bill was more than a brother to him and his parents were the two people that he thought of as his parents. They were the two people that were there to help him during his darkest moments. John Mueller was content spending his life with Paula, whose tender spirit and love for him tamed his rebellious nature and brought peace and balance to his life. The sun was setting in the west, the sky golden and bright. Soon another day would surrender its existence into the pitiless embrace of unforgiving time. He held Paula's hand. Next, to her, the time had reached infinity. They looked at each other and smiled. John Mueller was convinced that after all that he had lived and loved, she had become his other self. It is love that surpassed all other feelings and emotions.

Trails of Tragedy and Triumph

26

A FULL CIRCLE

Art Bauer had a difficult time adjusting to the civilian life. He was struggling to justify the death and atrocities of war. Everything he was taught from his young age as a boxer and later on in the military was intended to harden his mentality of harm or get harmed. Even when he slept, he would dream of people gasping their last breath in agony. There were airplanes crashing against mountains amidst dark smoke and fire and holes full of dead bodies with flocks of blackbirds descending from the gloomy skies.

It wasn't only the suffering of the adventure in Yugoslavia, but when in combat his fingers were always on the trigger; there was no soul, nor emotion, only one thing was on his mind; retaliation. There were other components of his young life rooted deep in his mind. For instance, his grandmother's moonshine and bootlegging. It was natural that Art Bauer opened a barroom in Huntington, West Virginia. Art Bauer was in his element: Epic fights, gunshots, limitless alcohol, tough women and illegal gambling. It was a place of familiarity for Art.

Dorothy Murray's family owned a full service thoroughbred horse breeding farm in Massachusetts. When Shaun O'Brien returned to Boston to married Dorothy, there was an elaborate wedding ceremony in the family farm. After their honeymoon, Shaun's father-in-law Daniel Murray proposed that the newlyweds stay on the farm and learn the art and science of breeding horses. The thirty acres farm was established by Daniel's grandfather. Shaun and Dorothy stayed to live and work on the farm, learning the business. They lived a busy life in the farm. They were playing tennis, taking long horse rides, breeding horses and babies. They had five children, two boys and three girls.

It was Saint George's day in Sparta, Greece. People came from the surrounding villages for the big event. This was the birthplace of Yiannis and Eleni Yiannopoulos. Their entire family flew in from New York City to celebrate the union of George and Ariana. The two met in Astoria. George was blinded by her beauty and a year later they were flying to Greece to get married. Ariana's ancestors came from the island of Kalymnos, the island chosen for their honeymoon. The ceremony was held outside since the church of Saint George was too small to handle the masses attending the wedding. Shortly after the ceremony, the sounds of klarino and bouzouki urged the people to circle and the dancing of the kalamatiano and tsamiko began. Soon there was a panegyric atmosphere, like the village in Yugoslavia, but here there was a full band of musicians with two singers and roasts on the spit. There was plenty of wine and ouzo, and tables laden with foods. When the sun rose the next day, there was still dancing, ouzo and eating. It was a day to remember.

Shortly after Clark Bailey was released from the service, he received a letter from Italy. The sender's name was Angela

Bruno, after reading the letter he realized that this was Maria's real name. They corresponded often over the next two years. Clark Bailey had no plans when he bought a ticket to Florence. He just had the urge to go to Italy.

When in Florence, he knew he was in a historical place. It was here that after one thousand years of darkness, the rediscovery of Greek philosophy and the merging of amazing artists and scientists. They once again enlightened the world. It was in this very city that the Renaissance began, and classical philosophy triumphed over theological bickering. Clark hired a taxi and asked the driver to take him to the address written on the mailing envelope. It was a forty-five-minute drive to the countryside. Rows of grapevines and olive tree groves unfolded between the unending hills. Along the olive and the vine, there were ruined castles and stone-built homes. The rolling green hills swept down to the coastal area into a long sandy beach. He went past a few seaside villages to a road lined with pine and cypress trees. The taxi driver drove off a path into a hillside which was embraced by more trees and facing the sea. They had arrived in Maremma, in Southwestern Tuscany and just south of the rugged Volterra hills. The driver stopped in one of the hillside villages, to ask some directions and then drove into the next village. He stopped by the small square and told Clark to wait there. "But this is not the address?" Clark was confused. "*Non preoccuparti amico. She come.*" Several minutes passed before Angela walked out from one of the narrow streets. Nervousness overcame Clark as he was questioning his decision to come here. But, Angela's cheerful "Ciao, Clark," her captivating smile and her warm embrace erased any doubts. After spending ten days in Italy with Angela, she decided to come and live in America.

Trails of Tragedy and Triumph

27

THE REUNION

Art Bauer's old barroom expanded into an established sports-bar with video games, a pool table, sports on television and offered a limited menu of tasty foods. It was a Tuesday evening on April 2nd, 1974 - past five-o-clock. Several police officers walked into Art's place and asked the bartender to stop pouring liqueur and asked the patrons to leave the place. By now the happy hour customers had gone and Art and his staff were preparing for the evening crowd. Surprise caught Art.

"What is the problem?" he asked.

The officer who seemed to be in charge responded, "Your liquor license is being revoked for serving minors."

There was a heated argument between Art and the officers, reminiscent of that of his grandmother arguing with the officers who were confiscating her moonshine.

"What does a man have to do to get a drink around here?" The voice came from a man sitting in a wheelchair. After the initial surprise, Art realized who that man was.

"Andy!" his voice joyful, his face expression astounded.

He looked up to the couple pushing Andy Ryker; it was John Mueller escorted by a lady.

"John!" for a moment Art Bauer was uncharacteristically speechless. "Who is the pretty lady next to you?"

Art was now back to his usual charming self. "This is my wife, Paula" John responded.

"What is going on?" Art was pleased to see old friends but amazed that they were in his sports bar.

"Well, today is our thirtieth anniversary of Lucky Lady, being shut down," Andy clarified.

The police officers were now smiling. "There is no problem with your place Art. We had to empty the place for your surprise anniversary party," the officer in charge said.

"What party?" At that moment the front door opened and six more couples walked in. There was Chris Moody with Susan, Shaun O'Brien and Dorothy, Bob Pastorelli with Mary, George Poulos with Ariana, Manny Cardenas with Carmen and Clark Bailey with Angela. In the meantime there were more police officers outside, explaining the situation to the customers leaving the place and then hung a "Private Party" sign on the door.

After a depressing few years due to losing his legs, Andy Ryker slowly realized that he could use his disability to help others. Andy was now traveling across the country and speaking to groups of veterans suffering from a post-traumatic stress disorder. He had prosthetics for his legs, but when speaking, he used a wheelchair for visual effects. During the massacre in the valley of death, when a mortar bomb exploded below Andy Ryker's legs, he fell into darkness. Andy didn't feel the Germans picking him up and bringing him to the village among the captured woman and children. The Germans took their prisoners to their camp. Before leaving the village, they burned all the homes and took the livestock with them. As he was being transferred, Andy Ryker was at times in the space of haziness. The rest of the time was just darkness; he remembered nothing. In the German field hospital, Andy's legs were amputated.

The Germans kept several injured members of the armed forces with the plan to exchange them for their injured soldiers, kept by the allies. When he returned home on an injured prisoners of war exchange, Andy didn't leave his house for two years.

One of the first people he contacted was Art Bauer. The two of them had long conversations over the phone.

Art Bauer confessed to Andy that he had a difficult time also dealing with his demons. "I am fine when I am with people, but when I am alone, I go to this tormented space. I want to kill myself and others. The strange thing is that at moments like these I think about our adventure and all that we went through with our team and I feel the love and the camaraderie. I think if something happened to me all of you will be sad. And I think of Stoney, and you, Andy, who lost parts of your body, and my issues do not seem so bad."

Andy was feeling close to Art since he went through the same depression for a very long time. There were many times that he thought of taking his own life but, eventually learned to live with the mental pain and used his experiences to help others.

"Art, you could help so many people by using your story of survival."

Several months before the thirtieth-year anniversary of being shut down, Andy Ryker contacted the rest of the members and asked them to have a reunion to celebrate their survival, honor Bill Stoney and help Art Bauer. Manny Cardenas had the idea of how to empty the customers from the bar. He had climbed the ladder through the ranks and had become a police commissioner. Manny contacted the chief of police in Art's area, explained the situation and asked for a favor. Now the entire surviving team was in Art's place, exchanging stories, laughing and drinking. During the past thirty years, most of the survivors kept in touch with one another, but they were never in the same place together. Andy Ryker was living in his parent's home in Los Angeles. Chris and Susan Moody visited him several times. Chris and Susan kept hiking and skiing. Clark with Angela traveled the world Clark Bailey never forgot the invitation from Cardenas. He traveled to El Paso and after tasting the enchiladas prepared by Manny's mother, he told Manny, "*Disfruté la cocina de tu madre*" in perfect Spanish pronunciation. Manny was impressed "I learned to roll my tongue by learning Italian" Clark responded. After living in the United States for a while Clark and Angela moved back to Italy's wine country.

Everyone raised their class in a toast to Bill Stoney. There were sober voices and tears in John Mueller's eyes. Mueller, shortly after his marriage, moved to Washington state, started an antique business, bought a boat and took on fishing. However, He was never the same ever since Bill Stoney passed – He had lost a part of himself. George Poulos and his siblings had taking over the family business. All of them were married and had several children. They stayed in Astoria to raise their kids around Papou and Yiayia, who's sole purpose was to spoil their grandchildren.

Pastorelli started a business installing sound systems for music groups. Because of the outstanding quality of his work his business was constantly growing. Eventually, his two sons took over and turned the business into a multi-million dollar company. Bob and Mary moved back to Arizona and spent his days playing golf and poker in the Indian casinos. Bob and Mary cherished their role as Nonno and Nonna to their grandchildren and during the family gatherings, he made pasta, pork neck sauce, beef meatballs, and *pan di spagna*.

For all who survived, there were tormenting moments when pain and suffering crept into their psyche. Their traumatic experiences were part of their existence, but they managed to live productive and happy lives because they were surrounded by true love. These survivors who witness inhumane atrocities and lived through unimaginable suffering are the absolute proof that love conquers all.

Trails of Tragedy and Triumph

EPILOGUE

Eternal Dilemma

This book is about an American B24 bomber crew shot down in enemy territory while returning from a successful mission. The narrative recounts human tragedy and captures the triumph of the human spirit. These men's heroic run for freedom bonded them in life and death. They walked for over six-hundred miles, climbing steep mountains, running through the German-occupied valleys and into dangerous lands divided by vicious bands of guerrilla warfare. These brave Americans made their way with the generous help of people who spoke a language that they could not understand. They were surrounded by famine and human misery and walked on land-mine infested territories. There were days of starvation, unbearable exhaustion, crossfires, bombings, and death. Despite these impossible odds, most of them made it through. Others did not.

This book is also a tribute to all unsung heroes who engaged in the controversial conflict we call war. It is about the men and women who came from the ranks of civil societies, who left families and jobs behind, to fight in the wars that others created. It is about those who now history refers to with the anonymous word "troops." Consequently, the eternal question remains unanswered; Should glory and victory surpass catastrophe and human suffering?

I believe that wars demonstrate a chain of events that intertwine into a maze of disastrous outcomes. In wars, the destiny of those involved is determined by the simple gesture of somebody else using a mechanism that is alien to our wishes and our will. My friend, look at those butchered in wars. Anyone of them could have been your son, your daughter. These are your children sent to wars by those who have the privilege to hold the ultimate power, a power that is used capriciously to display absolute command. A power that splits men's brains into a schizophrenic personality; one side talks about democracy, peace, and progress. The other side acts to destroy, to kill, to possess. It is that side that sends our sons and daughters to unfamiliar and pitiless places; to Stalingrad, to Iwo Jima, to Normandy, to Vietnam, to places where they arrive at field hospitals without legs, without arms, traumatized for life. As long as humans create wars, the concept of killing to survive will remain unchanged and unchangeable; Yesterday, today, tomorrow, forever.

War is a subject that this writer must explore in all of its aspects, its possibilities, and its consequences. As a writer, I must examine and understand why wars have transformed glory and legend into tragedy and chaos. War opens a box full of enigmas, a labyrinth of mixed feelings and unpredictable reactions. The danger that always exists is a story that repeats itself, a story that remains unexamined.

I've always had the seductive urge to write books in which the story talks about human feelings. This book is about the heroes who we will never hear about because they are on the stage for a short time, because they are insignificant in the bigger scope of history. Their names must be in the narrative of the eternal story of the person who, in war, manifests himself in all his truth because nothing reveals as much as wars. Nothing exacerbates with the same strength, beauty, and ugliness. Nothing else but wars unmasks our courage and our cowardice. It is difficult for me to fully comprehend what oratorical or psychological shrewdness persuades people to kill, to destroy, to devastate. Countless writers use World War II as a prototype to chronicle other wars. World War II was an event full of ideologies and feelings, a war that covered reality and fantasy without separating them. It was a time that the whole population of this planet was affected.

A war with deep roots of hate. A poisonous feeling that motivated the gangsters of Germany, Italy and Japan to conspire in an attempt to destroy the world. With aggression, human feelings are muted, and priority is given to resentment. It is a time when people become enemies and feel nothing for one another. Wars do that. Wars drain away all that makes one human.

Even those who did not witness the death camps, the killing of children, the torture and rape, are still mentally brutalized by the images of unbelievable human suffering. Because of that, we have lost a part of our being.

When the fighting finally ended, there was a chasm between those who read about the war and those who witnessed the brutalities, a chasm that never closed. It is true that this writer cries and laughs between the lines of the written word, and relives the events in a way that affects every dimension of his existence. But it is impossible to enter the realm of the spirit of those who physically experienced the fear of death and the exultation of victory. It is impossible to capture the dreams they dreamed and the nightmares they woke with.

In the realm of logic, we who never witnessed their suffering will be forever strangers to those who were brutalized. Brutalization, rape, torture, and any other severe suffering are kinds of pain that remain concealed within the compounds of shame, a feeling that rarely is shared with others.

This writer is left with the task to uncover the pain that wars have created. This writer does not want to see a repetition of World War II, a realization that came after seeing the civilian population wake up from the sleep of aggression and nothingness, to finally see the truth of the terrible results of warfare. A truth that has resulted in a wave of pacifism, a wave that has grown in volume, one that has created a generation that is shouting in a strong voice against military aggressiveness. A voice that will not leave the civilized nations intellectually naked, a voice that will not give in to the warlords who arm their bandits.

Today, in the aftermath of countless narratives of this eternal story called World War II, we can understand what happened in the trenches. Now it is time to leave the recounting of wars to the historians who so brilliantly illustrate them.

The time has come to examine the consequences of war, to stop the cannons ready to flare up their fire. A fire that has already consumed tens of millions of men, women, and children all over the world. For those who oppose the killing and bombings, it has been a ferocious battle to stop the bloodshed for peace and equal co-existing. It is a battle that will allow us to discover the inevitability of destiny and provide us with the formula of life. A formula I have no reason to doubt exists.

Nikos Ligidakis

Trails of Tragedy and Triumph

About the Author

Award winning author, Nikos Ligidakis, writes with clarity and passion in an ardent voice, not to just recount adventures, but with an expression of feelings, to encourage the reader to think, to find hope in the eternal suggle for the meaning of life and the awareness of harmony.

His culinary books, 5024 E. McDowell, A Man's Journey Into Culinary Exploration and My Private Collection of Pieces of Art, Dessert Recipes of A Master, Ligidakis demonstrates his priceless culinary knowledge, gained during his days as a celebrated chef.

Power and Defiance, The Human Struggle for Social Justice, it is the book Ligidakis calls, "The work of my lifetime." It is a labor of love, a nearly eight hundred page saga about the integrity of individual freedom and the intense struggle for social justice. Such deep matter requires not only the profound thoughts in writing but also the equal reflective thoughts in the reading.

The Extraordinary Life of Bill O'Brien, An Ordinary Arizona Irish Cowboy, is an inspirational story of adventure, excitement, achievement, the importance of character and how an "ordinary Arizona Irish Cowboy" overcame obstacles and challenges to achieve success in unique and creative ways. An entertaining and compelling narrative about one of Arizona's most fascinated characters.

His latest book, The Power of His Brush, The Evolution of R.C. Gorman, is a biography of the legendary Native American painter, Rudolph Carl Gorman. Born into poverty on the Reservation in Chinle, Arizona, R.C. Gorman was not expected to survive. However, under the nurture of his grandmother and others, this visionary Navajo distinguished himself as an extraordinary artist in the midst of a world dominated by white men. As the result of thousands of hours of research, Ligidakis has uncovered a story deeper than Gorman's bigger-than-life persona. With 85 images of Gorman's art, this hard-cover book will increase your understanding and appreciation of both the man and his work.

In Trails of Tragedy and Triumph, his tenth book, Ligidakis introduces a group of heroes in a fascinated story of survival during World War II. This incredible story narrates their attempt to freedom by running hundreds of miles in an enemy territory full of danger, exhaustion, starvation, and death.

Nikos Ligidakis

www.ingramcontent.com/pod-product-compliance
Lightning Source LLC
Chambersburg PA
CBHW030529100426
42813CB00001B/197